Transpiration

"Poetry and storytelling are the conduits of human refinement. They not only connect us to our past but open and propel us to our future."

Victor Anderson

Transpiration

Poetry and Storytelling as Our Spiritual Portals

Cornelia Benavidez

Megalithica Books
Stafford England

Transpiration: Poetry and Storytelling as Our Spiritual Portals
by Cornelia Benavidez
© 2018 First edition

Editor: Louise Coquio
Layout: Storm Constantine
Cover Design: Peter Hollinghurst

All photos are from the author's personal collection and were taken by her unless otherwise stated in the text.

ISBN: 978-1-912241-08-8
MB0200

Set in Book Antiqua

A Megalithica Books Publication
An imprint of Immanion Press
info@immanion-press.com
http://www.immanion-press.com

A Special Dedication

For my husband's brother Vice Admiral James H. Doyle Jr.
Whose kind words and support made this book possible.

Also:

To our families of body
That have loved and nurtured us.

To our families of heart
That embraced and encouraged us.

To our families of the spirit
That guide and uphold us.

And to the Lady Muse
Who impassions and inspires our journey.

Transpiration

Transpire: To come to light, to come about; revealed, happen or occur. To come out of, to change.

> *Transitive verb*: To become known or be disclosed.

> *Physiology*: transitive and intransitive verb: to give off water vapor through the pores of the skin.

> *Botany*: transitive and intransitive verb: to lose water vapor from a plant's surface, especially through surface spore stomata.

Transpiration: The act or process of transpiring, to pass over to something else.

> 15th century: the act or process or an instance of transpiring, especially the passage of watery vapor from a living body (as of a plant) through a membrane or pores.

> A fluid filtered transference from one state to another.

Contents

A Few Words on the Purpose of This Book

For some, the writing of poetry or autobiographical material are both considered to be somewhat self-indulgent processes. Yet I say that the sharing of our adventures, thoughts and creative flights of fancy, passion and history, give us an inside look at others and confirmation of our shared human experience. It can also provide windows and doorways to areas inside our own awareness and intellect, where one has not yet fully personally explored or resolved. We are all explorers after all; from the child digging into the earth to see what she or he can find, to the daring adult who sets sail to parts unknown. This seeking process that moves us in our human journey of travelling and rooting about, is not just a physical process, but an intellectual, emotional and spiritual one as well. It leads us to revisit the known territories within ourselves, or to push our boundaries into the new and unexplored.

All people wish and endeavor to be understood and to test boundaries for themselves. We desire to investigate and affirm what is true, for life is full of theories, possibilities and mysteries. Storytellers, poets, scientists and adventurers all mine for their own kind of gold and, when they find it, their triumph is not just in the eureka of the find, but the joy of sharing the journey as well. In sharing with others, we are not just entertaining one another, but teaching others the joys and perils of the quest, be they internal or external. Perhaps one reason we have the drive to quest so bravely is to satisfy our hope of the other realities and possibilities available to us in life and beyond.

In this work are some of the highlights of my own journey. My own experiences, and the things they have taught me, which have shaped my creativity and spiritual leanings. I hope that my journey from childhood to the present makes you smile and encourages you to love in the face of our complex human existence. Most of all, I hope it teases your heart to write and speak of your own journey of experience and discovery.

Cornelia Benavidez
November 2018

Introduction

The Poet, Storyteller and Bard is the Visionary, Artist, Dreamer, Shaman, Healer and Weaver of so many traditions around the world. Poets walk into the physical and psychological darkness to find answers to common problems, as well as to uncover the spiritual truths that uphold the present and inspire the future.

In modern times, we are fervently urged to seek answers to our questions in 'how to' books, as well as through institutional mouthpieces, be they through traditional news, morning and afternoon television or special documentaries, all expressing their statistical conclusions. Those queries have their place, yet the human heart longs for the esoteric and the romantic; for an art of ideals that thrills the soul. Thus, seekers have turned to poetry in its many forms. Those seekers, whoever they may be, are from all faiths, paths and perspectives. They frequently seek poetry's wisdom and often become its next creators. For them, the experience of poetry's unique role may begin at birth, but more often it is something that happens to them over time, gradually emerging as the individual walks their own path. Poetry's unfolding process occurs in life experience, during dreamtime and in the workings of the imagination. It finally blossoms through the guidance of the Muse and her teachers.

Poetry's inspirational spark is found in the blood of all those who are called to journey those roads of the human spirit. Perhaps the poetic process also springs from a soul's deep acceptance of a larger reality outside of organic form. It generates the need to portray, with words and song, the expressions of the heart and endeavors to adequately describe the expansion of the mind as well as the whispers and flashes of our possible experiences of the Divine realms. This by some is called enlightenment.

This book attempts a broad scope in the exploration of poetry in its many guises and uses in my own life. These are the paths of my personal journey that led to the growth of my spirit. In most of these stories I have used real names, and in some 'close names' – if I am not in touch with the person or they have passed on. It is here, I believe, in stories and poetry, that we connect to the wellspring of imagination and the mysteries of life generating the growth of all human souls. Hereby I hope to offer some insights, guidelines and inspiration to those who want to peruse and pursue poetry's sacred arts.

Cornelia Benavidez (Doyle)

My Family History

Throughout my life there were key moments when storytelling and poetry played a role in shaping me. Both sides of my family came from a long line of salt of the earth, hardworking people. Woven into this tapestry were artists, dancers, mystics, and storytellers. My father played the accordion and could literally sing the birds right out of the trees. His Spaniard father's family history has deep roots in the lore of both the new and old worlds, the latter going back to Christian mystics and a touch of royalty, but mostly to the ancient Basque people. This history, as I later came to learn, was much more complex than that which I'd initially perceived. Papa's father I never met. I had always thought he was just Spaniard and Mexican Indian, like many people of Mexican decent are in both Mexico and all of the Americas. I grew up to learn that there are so many more tribes then what I had seen in cowboy movies and on television as a child. I came to understand that some are like a chain of distant cousins, while other tribes can have very different histories – genetic testing supports this. It turned out that Papa's native genes, mostly from his Mother, were the Totonaca, and a drop of Mayan yet they also spread upwards to United States to include tribes of the American southwest. Another ancestral line wove its way South, all the way to Peru. What connected many of these tribes was their lore and love of birds, especially the eagle, which may explain our family's admiration of birds of prey.

My father's Spanish line broke into two main branches. One was predominantly Iberian Celt, which is mostly Basque with a little French. The other, with its ancient royal roots, spread back to Alfonzo the Eleventh in Spain and further to many places; including traces way back to old Egypt, with a few drops of Jewish and Persian. Thrown into the pot there is even a drop of Irish leading back to an ancient king.

Some of my Spanish ancestors were among the first here in the New World. They were everything from aristocratic mayors to cardinals that founded towns from Mexico to Santa Fe. They made tiles, brewed beer and, if not Catholic, were known as mystical spiritual people. Sadly, I never got to know my father's father because he passed away. Mama Martina gave birth to Papa in Texas and then remarried there. I feel very lucky that I did get to know her. My Spanish was never as good as my German, so it was mostly from Papa I would hear her family stories. She told of a French explorer who came to the New World and married into her tribe. Her family was long known in Mexico for being healers and storytellers. She herself was known for singing old Native and Spanish songs. While she endlessly picked cotton in Texas, she would sing, passing along old folk tales and family history. Therefore, it was many who called her Mama Martina. Martina was the last name she was given as a child - my grandmother's native name was long taken from her family by the government and church, but she fiercely held on to her stories, just as my German grandmother did.

Mama Martina

My German mother was almost eleven years old when the Second World War began rearing its ugly head in the lovely small provincial town where she lived. Her father had picked up the family and had left the beautiful northern port city of Königsberg in east Germany, where my mother and her sister had been born. She was a little girl when they moved to western Germany, to the small bucolic spa town of Bad Kreuznach, where they hoped to avoid the growing political unrest. Fearing another war, they had moved to this small town hoping to have a more peaceful and safer life for their girls. It was a valiant attempt, but people were only safer high up in the mountains. My mother and other children risked the dangerous train ride to be housed and to work at the mountain farms during the worst of the bombing. Her father had served in WWI and he was at first relieved that he was too old to serve, but in the long run my Opa knew better. He told my mother that those coming to power were heating up the blood of the people by either telling lies or confusing them. He managed to protect his family and stay out of the war's way for a while, but then they came for every healthy male they could find. First, young able men, then still healthy veterans and those boys that were fourteen to sixteen. In the end they snatched up the old that could still stand and boys as young as ten. Opa ended up in a Russian prison camp and was very lucky to make it back home alive after torture and terrible hardship. Oma, my grandmother, was head of the Red Cross in her community and my mother would assist her. She had to grow up quickly. She told me and my sister that one day she and her family were living a lovely life and in two days everything changed. It was not just her way of life but every part of it as the Nazis pushed their way into the newspaper, radio, school even the bakery in her small town. Nothing was the same.

Kreuznach Brueckenhaeuser (River Houses)

Mother's classical piano teacher lived in the house to the far left. I spent time there in 1960 looking out of the Bay Window. The pointy tower is now gone, I think.

Even when the war was not on her doorstep, with bombs raining on her head, she, her mother and sister lived a life of super vigilance every day – from starving people, or those driven mad by pain, as well as Nazis looking for meds or a place to sleep. For women and children, there was the never-ending threat of rape by soldiers from all sides.

My mother was almost seventeen when the war ended. Then came the *Great Starvation*, a time of mass suffering that was both physical and emotional. In various ways, the German people now discovered not only all the unseen horrors of the war, but also how they had been lied to and manipulated to be either innocent, confused partners or else co-conspirators in a national nightmare of horror so profoundly evil that it was totally numbing to mind and spirit. My mother and grandmother found out about Auschwitz from one of my mother's school mates. He was only fifteen and already a soldier. He had been shot in the shoulder and was told to go home. Hitching rides in hay carts and ox carts he ended up going by the town of Auschwitz. He saw the billowing smoke of much burning coming out of the towers and smelled the awful stench that hung in the air. He asked the farmers what was going on and they told him to just go home. The courage and curiosity of the young is powerful, so he managed to get close enough to call out to a ragged man by a barb-wired fence.

'You, foolish boy!' called back the man, 'Go back! They will kill you, Germans die here too.'

'Who dies here?' called out the boy.

'Everyone! Men, women, children, mostly Jews but also others. All are burned in the towers! Run boy, run! Tell your family, anyone who will listen what you saw and smelled here!'

The boy made it back to my mother's house at midnight, days later, with a stolen bottle of wine and a fever, which my grandmother treated. He told them everything and they drank the wine and cried together till the wee hours of the morning.

Yet, despite all that my mother and her family witnessed and suffered throughout the war, she and my grandmother were determined to find and hold on to fleeting moments of joy or beauty, be it making a beautiful dress out of the taffeta lining of some curtains (very much like that famous scene in *Gone with the Wind*), or by playing boogie-woogie on the piano as an act of rebellion, and later by dancing ballet in a circus as all the theaters had been bombed. My mother's roots, after all, stemmed from a hearty stock spread deep all over eastern and northern Germany and beyond. On her father's side they had come down from Sweden, Finland and some from the Laplander-Sami people. Opa was raised Lutheran but he also was very philosophical with a deep respect for the philosophies and teachings of Rudolf Steiner and Carl Jung. Both my Grandparents loved fairy-tales and folklore of all cultures. On my grandmother's side were very ancient Germanic roots with a sprinkling of people from Austria, Lithuania and Northern Italy, as well as a drop of Roma (Gypsy people) and even a trace of Welsh from far away Wales. Oma could speak many languages and was known not only for her nursing skills, but for her flair as an herbalist and her love of animals.

I lived in Germany from the age of four to five but, when I was eight years old, my grandmother came to live with us in Albion Michigan for nearly a year. She called me her beloved Gypsy girl or her Hawaiian girl, I think because of my long, dark, wind-blown hair. We explored woods and cornfields, while she told me her tales of the horrors of war and the truths of spirit that sustained her. She was the first to tell me that most Christians do not understand that the world is full of many possibilities and miracles. She told me about the Good Hexen (good witches) and how they and Mystical Christians like the Gnostics were so brutally killed by the Catholics. She told me that her ancestors became part of a group that had fled the Catholic persecutions. They were saved by a King in Northern Germany who said; 'I do not care if you are Jewish, Protestant, Pagan or Gnostic or whatever. As long as you are not Catholic you are welcome.'

My Oma told me that many people, not just her family, were or became Protestant but still practiced some of the customs of the old ways. Housewives exchanged knowledge, skills and superstitions over fences and in sewing circles for hundreds of years, helping their families to survive through endlessly changing politics and local conflicts. Oma taught me that all people, no matter who they are, can fall into temptation. The Priest or Minister must stand for his people before God and plead for forgiveness for their sins. The Hexen steps into the crossroads of fate and attempts to change or turn its course with his or her appeals. Both are necessary, both can work for good or evil. Grace and wisdom are what is needed to shield both from temptation. It was all very heady stuff for such a young child.

My mother and father met in Bad Kreuznach after Germany had begun to recover from the Second World War. It is one of our family's romantic tales, which I knew were true, because I'd hidden under tables, listening to the adults talk as a small child. My father had been a soldier stationed in Germany. He had seen a poster advertising my mother performing Spanish flamenco dancing in a theater. He thought she might be Northern Spanish, especially since her hair-dressing made her blond hair look darker. He told his friend that he was going to find her and marry her. He found out that she was German and that she lived with her parents. So, he showed up under her bedroom

Cornelia Benavidez

window with his accordion and a guitarist and sang Spanish love songs, followed by others in every language he knew. He wooed her, and her parents, for two years before finally having a true fairytale wedding.

Mutti and Papa's wedding

Eventually my parents returned to the United States with blessings and encouragement from my Grandparents. They first went to my father's home in Texas where I was born. My mother worked as a nurse while my father completed his service. Between two and three years old, we moved to Michigan, so that my father could take advantage of the factory boom there. My father also remembered that he had made a solemn promise to my mother's father that, after four to five years, he would send my mother home with any child they might have. So, this was how I met my grandparents, aunt and cousin and learned the German culture. It was from here that my journey begins, as I share with you snapshots of my life, where storytelling and poetry began to create the woman I would become.

Tender Beginnings

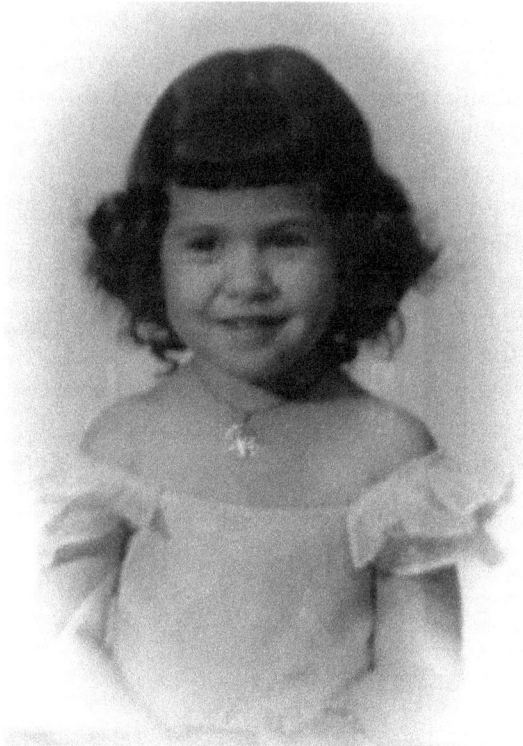

Me between the ages of two and three

I was out in the garden with my grandfather, who called to me.

'Let me show you something,' he said, taking me to a flowering bush of pink bleeding hearts. Carefully pinching off a delicate blossom, he showed the heart-shaped little thing barely the size of a nickel in his palm. 'Here is the flower as the hand of God and Nature made it.'

'I thought only God makes everything, Opa' I questioned.

He smiled, winked, and with a chuckle said, 'They are

an old married couple, I think.' He turned his back to me for about thirty seconds, and when he turned around again his palm was open. There in his hand was a perfect tiny Flamingo bird with one leg up and a curved graceful neck and head.

'Opa!' I cried. 'It's like magic.'

'Yes, it *is* like magic,' he explained. 'But it is even more so like art.'

I looked closely at how fragile and perfect the little flower bird was in his palm. 'Opa, I do not think I can ever do this art,' came my sad response.

Again, he smiled and said, ever so gently, 'You are human, so you're meant to be an artist. Some people have a kind of blindness, so they do not understand this. You, my child, may never make flamingos out of blossoms, but you will find the art in you, just like your mother did.'

I beamed and asked, 'So I will play the piano or dance like Mutti, or sing like Papa?'

Opa nested the little flower bird in a rose near the house. 'Perhaps, or maybe you'll draw or paint or write or build things. That is what life should be about, finding the best artist inside yourself.'

My Opa and Oma and a happy me

Later, with a child's enthusiasm, I dragged my mother to see the little flamingo in his rose nest.

My mother smiled and asked, 'Did Opa tell you, listening to nature and doing art brings one closer to God.'

'Closer than praying?' I responded with surprise.

She laughed. 'Music, Poetry and Nature is how God talks to our hearts, and we, by our art, answer back.'

I never forgot those words, or that flamingo, and whenever I see a bleeding-heart bush, the memory comes rushing back. From that moment on, I wondered what kind of art was in me. It has taken a lifetime to explore, and like my roots, it has many branches.

The Church, the Painting
and the Child

The church in my hometown was a giant monument to
tasteful severity. Even its simple, square stained-glass
windows, with colors of yellow, light green, orange and
light blue, reflected this message. The aisle between the
plain hardwood pews seemed to me at least half a block
long or longer. My little feet, in their hard, black, patent
leather Mary Jane shoes, clicked down the spit-shined floor
with all the discretion a barely six-year-old could muster.
My mother, it seemed, was following some strict but
unwritten code of protocol, which insisted our little family
would march down the aisle, with casual unhurried grace,
to the third or fourth row from the front pew on the left,
thirty seconds to no more than one minute before the
Pastor would make his entrance. How this was all
arranged was a great childhood mystery for me. Our
pastor, in his flowing, angelic, hand-me-down robes,
would stride out from stage right, taking his place in front
of the large altar beset at both ends with beautiful flower
arrangements. Over him, and above all of us, loomed a
gigantic plain wooden cross, towering twenty or more feet
high. My father helped hang that cross, an almost
incomprehensible feat for my fledging three or so year-old
consciousness at the time. In the back, behind us, rose an
organ that was awesome in dimension as well as sound. Its
pipes of aqua blue steel surrounded the choir like a
protective (and at times overbearing) fortress. This was
God's house.

After the service, we would all file past the Pastor like
dutiful children before exiting into the foyer. The women
would smile, nod, and ask him about his wife or children,

while the men would extend a firm handshake and gruffly mutter, 'Good service' or 'Fine sermon.' I was expected to curtsy and get out of the way as soon as possible. If my parents tarried thereafter, I would have time to dash to the waiting room. Once there, I'd stare at my favorite painting in the whole church before being shooed to the cloakroom. The waiting room was set up like a very large living room with scattered sofas and coffee tables. On the walls were various paintings of Jesus throughout his life but my favorite one, 'Jesus and the Children,' was a little unique. Every Sunday I looked forward to catching a glimpse of it and, if I was lucky, I would have time to kneel on the sofa underneath it to look up and examine its every detail with the earnest care of childlike wonder and curiosity.

I am not quite sure what started my fascination with the painting. There were other such paintings in the room, much more dramatic or heavenly looking in their golden tones. These included Jesus as a child in the temple, Jesus and the fishermen, the Last Supper, Jesus praying, and Jesus on the cross. These others mostly held little interest for me, however. Perhaps it could have been that, as a child myself, I was relating to the children in the painting. Yet now, as the memories come back to me, I recall also how 'Jesus and the Children' made me feel. It was a large long painting, yet it had a gentle commanding presence. On one side sat Jesus surrounded by children in biblical clothes, but his arms were stretched out towards children that were running toward him from the other side of the painting. Those children were dressed in modern clothes and their faces were filled with joy as they dashed across the canvas. To stand in front of it was to behold a promise of total love and affection. I too wanted to meet Jesus, ask him a few questions, and hopefully get a hug and feel his love as well. The painting seemed to say that this was not only as it should be, but possible for me as well. The dominant pastel colors of blue and violet gave the scene an almost fairytale or other-worldly quality. It occurred to me, even at that tender age, that maybe this dreamlike world in the painting was the way we really all should live, or that this was maybe God's real world in heaven. It may well have been this very thought that first sprouted the seeds of my spiritual questing. Yet, at the tender age of six, there was only one source of truth for me, and that was Mutti (German for Mommy). As far as I was concerned, Papa worked for God, the Pastor spoke for God, but Mutti had, I was sure, deep profound conversations with him. So, one Sunday after a quick review of the painting in the church, when we were back home, I followed her about the kitchen, before asking;

'Mutti?'

'Yes, child?' she queried, in that lilting, light German accent I loved so well.

'Mutti, did Jesus really have blue eyes?'

'We do not know for sure.' She smiled.

I decide to press the point. 'We seem to know so much about Jesus and his life and almost all the pictures have him with blue eyes except for one. There he has golden eyes.'

'Well, that is because many of the artists who paint these pictures come from countries where most people have blue eyes. You see, my child, everyone wishes that Jesus would look just like one's own people, so the good father in heaven made sure that we would never exactly know. Then no one can be jealous,' my mother responded in her most reasonable tone.

'Maybe,' I brightened, 'that is why the one artist painted Jesus with gold eyes because no one has them!'

'No...' she corrected me gently, 'Gold eyes are rare, but people can have them. When I was a little girl, I had a friend who we named Amber after the stone because of her golden eyes.'

'Oh,' I said, slightly deflated. I inched closer to Mutti,

looking into her deep green eyes with my brown ones and said, 'Blue eyes are beautiful because they are the color of the sky and heaven so maybe Jesus did have blue eyes.'

My mother took a deep breath. 'Brown is beautiful too. It is the color of earth itself, of the trees and the eyes of the deer in its forest.'

I smiled broadly, as I had never quite thought of it that way. 'And your eyes, Mutti? What are your eyes like?'

She laughed heartily, 'They are the eyes of the eagle and the cat and, at night, the owl that sees everything,' she answered, tickling me.

I squealed and giggled but I knew that this was undoubtedly true.

The next Sunday after church my parents were part of a luncheon held for some committee. Come to think of it, in those years, at those church luncheons, I must have seen every possible combination of Jell-O. Such as Jell-O and fruit, Jell-O and veggies and Jell-O with cake and cream. For some reason green was the traditional color for much of this fare. We children would brace ourselves for the sweet, cheek-pinching little old ladies, who were totally convinced that the only reason children behaved in church or Sunday school was for the happy promise of heaping dancing spoonfuls of green, possibly red Jell-O with suspended bits of questionable et cetera. So, after swallowing several green spoonfuls, to the satisfaction of those around me, I stole away and scampered upstairs to the waiting room.

I was thrilled to have the time to study the painting with no distractions or, hopefully, interruptions. I stood squarely in front of it, even risking standing on the sofa. My eyes focused on one little girl. She was in a pink dress, with a pink ribbon band in her hair, and she was running toward Jesus ahead of the rest of the children. It occurred to me then that this painting was different from all the rest, not just in this room but in the whole church. It was the only picture that portrayed people from our time. Realizing this fully further strengthened my belief that there must be a secret within this painting, maybe even a secret way to see Jesus!

Oh boy! I thought, *maybe this is something like the secrets of Santa Claus? Christmas is Jesus's birthday after all.*

I looked at the painting with new eyes, feeling butterflies in my tummy.

How good of a girl will I have to be to be to be able to talk to the Son of God? Let alone to sit in his lap.

Now to think of this as something that was actually possible was a little intimidating. I bit my lip, sitting down and thinking hard.

How good does one have to be to get to see Jesus now? Where is Jesus now? . . . Jesus is in heaven with . . . That's it! This must be the answer or maybe part of it. These children have just arrived in heaven! Yet, after all, everyone knows you dress like in angel robes or bible-type clothes when you are in heaven. Yes, I thought with hopeful confidence, *these children must have just arrived because they are dead children. Baptized dead children, to be exact.*

I let this thought roll about my head while I climbed back on the sofa to take a renewed and closer look.

Maybe, if I examine each child's face something might betray how he or she died. There are so many of them, maybe they all died on a bus or train. No, that can't be . . . they all seem to be dressed in their Sunday best clothes with perfect hair and all look so healthy and happy, especially that little girl in the pink dress. No, these can't be dead children because no matter how beautiful heaven is, and how sweet Jesus must be, if I had just been smooshed by a crashed bus I would at the very least look a little, ah, unsettled and worried about my family. I am sure Jesus would understand.

I climbed off the sofa.

All these pictures are supposed to be true, and that's why they are hanging in church. Maybe I can find a clue in the other paintings hanging in the room. Maybe, I could have missed something.

I slowly circled the room.

Jesus and his disciples, Jesus praying, Jesus and the sheep... wait a minute!

I took a closer look at this painting. There was Jesus and, in the background, and there were lots of sheep, but He really did not look like a shepherd with such nice robes and that big golden halo around his head and shoulders.

Wait a minute! The sheep he's holding has a halo too! Why is that?

A strange idea flashed into my head and I dashed off.

I ran back downstairs, peeking about and looking for Mutti. Not seeing her, I took a chance and, to my delight, found her alone in the bathroom freshening her lipstick and make-up.

'Mutti?' I said, a little breathlessly.

'Yes, my little May bug?' (Believe me it sounds much better in German)

'Sheep have brown eyes, right?' I asked.

'Yes,' she replied patiently then arched an eyebrow and stood straight, looking into the mirror. 'At least I think most of them do.'

I continued. 'Most people have brown eyes. Yes?'

'Yes, most people in the world have brown eyes. What is this all about, child? Are you still trying to figure out how Jesus looked?' She searched for her powder compact in her purse.

'Mutti, how do people paint things or people that they have never seen like Jesus? They make it so real.'

'Well... there is more than one answer for this, my child. Talented people can sometimes have more than one gift or talent.' Mutti powered her nose and continued. 'Besides being able to draw and paint they might have a very strong imagination, giving them a vision of what things or people may have looked like.'

'But I thought that when you say it's your imagination it means it's not true.' My head tilted to the side, my brow furrowed as I gazed up at her.

'Yes, that is so, but people have to be careful because *inspiration* and *imagination* are very close together. People sometimes have dreams that they are sure are from God and some feel that when you choose to paint things from the Bible the angels guide your hand.' She had finished powdering her nose and was now looking for her mascara.

'Do you think that is how it happens, Mutti?' I asked.

She paused momentarily and took a deep breath before speaking. 'I can't really say. I've never tried to paint a picture of Jesus.'

I was somewhat surprised that there was anything that my mother might lack in knowledge or skill. 'You draw animals very real,' I said to her brightly.

'Animals and people are two very different things.' She started carefully blackening her lashes with the tiny brush at the end of the stick.

I, though, wanted to return to my point, so I flatly stated, 'Mutti, I think Jesus is a sheep.'

'What!?' My mother burst out with a laugh, then quickly reached for a tissue to repair a slight smudge.

'Even the Pastor says so and, in the painting upstairs, Jesus has a halo and the sheep has a halo,' I added triumphantly.

'Lamb.' My mother broke into a big smile. 'You mean Lamb of God. Jesus was a Lamb of God, not a sheep,' she admonished me, dabbing at the corners of her eyes and trying to keep her composure.

'That's right. Jesus is the Lamb of God. That's a baby sheep, right?'

'Right.'

My mind was working furiously. 'So, the Pastor said to us that Jesus is special because he is God's son and that is why he has a halo, which is a heavenly crown. Right?'

31

'Ah... Right.'

'And God does not have a wife, but he wanted a son, so he made one, like he did Eve, out of Adam's rib. But this time, because it's his boy he puts Jesus in Mary's tummy, so he could have a mother. Right?'

Mutti was looking a little wary but nodded. 'Right.'

'So, Jesus has a halo because he is God's son, but the Lamb has a halo because somehow, he is like Jesus. So maybe God turned a lamb into a little boy because lambs are sweet and have mostly brown eyes maybe sometimes blue, so Jesus then was a Lamb of God.' I grinned widely with the pleasure at having puzzled this all out. 'Right?'

'Well, you have a very interesting way of thinking about all this but, child, it is not so simple.' She put her makeup back into her purse and faced me.

'Why not?'

'Sometimes we have things that are true, but they are true by symbols. The lamb is a symbol of the sacrifice that Jesus made for us. Sheep give us their warm woolly coats to make clothes and many other things with. Sheep are the main food in many countries, like cows and chickens are here. It is not so easy to figure these things out because, like I said, God does not want us to have false pride or be jealous. Right?' Mutti said, in a very sympathetic tone.

I was not quite sure what false pride was but, suddenly, I felt very tired. Mutti herded me out of the door.

'There you are!' It was Papa; he had been looking for us. Papa bent down, eyeing me closely. 'Does she feel all right?' he asked my mother.

'Oh, she feels just fine, only tired,' answered my mother with a chuckle. 'Let's go home and we will talk more later.'

As I slipped off to sleep later that evening, I could hear the distant mumbling of my parents in the kitchen, then the roaring belly laugh of my father. I wondered what was so funny.

Bible School Lessons

The summer was full upon us and, as sure as Christmas came every year, so did summer Bible school. I was thinking of asking our Sunday school teacher some questions about the painting but felt a little put off by her imposing presence. She was a large box-shaped woman in her early fifties, always well dressed in elegant Sunday suits that somehow almost always matched one or the other stained-glass windows, so that it seemed she was just as much a part of the church as the pews or the pastor.

About six or seven of us children sat in little chairs lined up like birds on a wire. With great flourish and drama, she read us the story of Abraham and his little boy Isaac, who was going to be sacrificed on an altar upon a mountain by his father, because God had told him to. Then, in the last second the boy is spared, and some poor ram God tangled in a bush was killed instead. The teacher then asked how we liked this story.

Of course, I piped right up.

'I don't think I like this story. I don't really understand it.'

'What is it you don't understand, my dear?' The teacher beamed down on me like a lighthouse.

I took a deep breath. 'Well, why would God ask Abraham to kill his own boy when his commandment is "Thou shalt not kill?" It seems like a very cruel trick.'

'Very good question.' She continued to beam. 'This is because in those Old Testament days before Jesus, people showed God love by the willing sacrifice of their wealth or even themselves if God asked.'

'But God did not ask Abraham to kill himself!' I jumped in. 'And he did not even ask Isaac!' I turned to the children around me and asked, 'Did anybody hear God ask Isaac?' My fellow children looked at me owl-eyed and either shook their heads or shrugged their shoulders. I turned back to the teacher, who now had this stone frozen smile on her face, yet I bravely continued,

'I also do not understand why God tangled up a ram in a bush to be killed, because God does not have a body, so he does not eat. So why did this poor ram have to die?'

'Because, my dear, the whole point of the story is the value and respect given unto God through sacrifice!' She stated a little more loudly.

So I answered back somewhat meekly, 'But... but God said thou shall not kill and...'

'I know this is hard for children to understand,' she broke in. 'But this...' And the teacher stripped off her jacket, revealing the crisp white linen tank underneath, as well as the drop-down of her large, drooping, chicken wing upper arm flaps. She threw her arms open wide, like a winged Jesus on the cross. We children huddled together in astonishment and fear at what might come next.

'THIS!' she cried loudly. She reached across her mighty bosom and grabbed her sagging skin beneath her arms. With a tone of solemn finality, she announced: 'This! This is a waste of flesh!'

We were all frozen to our seats, mouths open, and from somewhere around me I heard a little sniffle.

The teacher lowered her arms with great dignity. She picked up her jacket and slipped it on, making her arms once again appear normal.

She spoke brightly once more. 'Well, there you have it, children. We may not understand the sacrifices God wishes from us, but we must be thankful for the rams he does send us. Have a wonderful rest of the day.' She flashed a broad smile.

After I was dropped home that day, I tore into the house, startling my mother folding laundry.

'Mutti! Mutti!' I cried. 'Are we a waste of flesh?'

'What?'' exclaimed my mother.

'Let me show you so you understand.'

I acted out the whole story and by the time I got to the dramatic flesh grab I threw off my light summer coat, put on my best Shirley Temple frown face and grabbed my little sausage arm. Attempting to sound furious, I cried out; 'This! This! Is a waste of flesh!''

I had never heard my mother laugh so loud. I thought she was going to tip right over. 'Child... Child, you will take to the stage one day I am sure of it!' She dabbed her eyes with her hanky.

'You mean like the movies?'' I asked, quite pleased.

'Maybe.' She shrugged. 'But the stage would be better, I think.' She started to laugh again as she sank into a chair.

'Mutti?' I asked softly as I gently tugged at her clothes. 'Do you talk to Jesus every day?'

My Mother buried her face in a larger handkerchief that she had pulled out of her skirt pocket and said in a muffled voice, 'Mothers are very busy people, so we ask the angels to help us watch over things and to ask God questions for us. I... talk to Jesus on Sunday like everyone else.'

'Oh, so when the pastor speaks to Jesus, is it in his office or the little room next to the altar?'

Mother's face came out of hiding with a happy grin. 'You will have to ask him and let me know... but remember that maybe he can't tell you. Like I told you before, speaking to God and Jesus is a very private thing.'

'It's because people might get jealous that you had seen and talked to Jesus, right?'

'Right.' She blew her nose.

'Can I talk to Jesus?'

'Every time you pray you are talking to him.'

'But I want to speak to him like I do to you, like the pastor does and like the children do in the painting.'

'What painting?' she asked.

'It's the painting of Jesus and the children in the church,

over the sofa. Jesus is there with children in Bible clothes and he is reaching out to children dressed like me.'

'Oh, I see, so you want to be like the children in the picture?'

'Right.' I nodded.

She gazed out into the air, then closed her eyes a moment before pulling me onto her lap.

'You see, my little bug, a painting is not like a photo. A photo is a picture almost always of something as it happens in real life, like what we see with our eyes. A painting, because it is art, can do so much more. Like poetry that can dress up plain words and make them more alive because of the rhyme or the rhythm, a painting does the same thing with color, tone and symbols. So, we don't have pictures of Jesus or people in Roman times, but we have all kinds of art and writings that give us an idea of what that time and its people may have looked like.'

'But this is different Mutti,' I quietly protested. 'There are children in Bible clothes and children in modern clothes. I thought maybe they were dead children at first… going to see Jesus in heaven but now I don't think so.'

'Cornelia, this artist is painting an idea, or a dream or wish. Maybe even a deep feeling,' she explained.

'Then you mean it's not true?' My eyes started to brim with tears. 'It's all just something made up in their head?'

'Oh child, child,' she sighed. 'This is one of those things that is both a yes and no. Please don't cry! You will have a red nose.' Mutti kissed my cheek in an effort to have me smile a bit. 'Remember what I told you about poetry? That it is a type of writing that colors words in a way that can then speak to our feelings? And paintings do that with colors? It is trying to show you something that is true like riddles and rhymes that hold secrets and so do paintings sometimes.'

'So, what is true in this painting Mutti?'

'What is true is that Jesus loved children very much. It says so in the Bible and even though it was a long time ago that Jesus lived on earth, all children in their hearts should run to him. This I think is the message of the painting.'

'I think you may be right, Mutti!' My face brightened up even more. 'Mutti? Do you think there still might be another secret message in the painting?'

'That could be, you never know,' she said sliding me off her lap. 'Maybe you will uncover it.'

Fully satisfied for the moment I ran to play.

The next Sunday I contemplated the picture anew. If there was another secret in this painting, what could it be, other than what now seemed so obvious? I was embarrassed that the answer had not hit me earlier. I scanned the picture fully, the trees, the grass and ground, the faces, the colors and tones, yet my eyes kept turning back to the little girl in the pink dress. Her feet barely touched the ground as she was running so fast, so full of joy, towards Jesus, while Jesus was reaching out to her, his face full of happiness so sweet, so perfect. Suddenly, I caught my breath! From somewhere a strange and wonderful thought came, tickling and expanding in my mind like an unfolding flower. My heart started to pound a little faster. I was filled with a glowing glee as my hands went up to my cheeks. I took a deep breath and knelt on the sofa, my hands folded, as I made a solemn pact with the painting that I would never tell its secret, not to anyone, adult nor child, until I felt the time was right.

I never did for the next 45 years. Yet then, I thought, how could I have missed it? The perfect honey-colored hair, the blue eyes and the joy that only a little girl can feel when she has been away from someone she loves so deeply. Yes, this is the painting's deeper secret: Even though Jesus loves all children throughout all time, he too has a little girl of his very own, just like my Papa does. Her spirit is always searching to run back to him and his waiting arms. But we can't talk about it, or even know for sure, because God would not want us to be jealous.

The Song of All Songs

As a child my world was filled with music. Due to this, soundtracks in movies seemed quite logical to me, and I was very aware of everyone's soundtrack in my neighborhood. They drifted in the wind and floated in through windows of houses and cars. It seemed that we moved to their sound all summer. When I was between ten and eleven, in our neighborhood, the two Italian families would play opera, romantic dance tracks and send their kids off to dance school. The Mexican kids cha-cha'd and Salsa'd and, in the local Armory we all learned to polka.

The Armories were in communities all over Michigan. This was where weapons and goods were stored in case of a local or national emergency. There was a large gym-sized room for wedding receptions and all kinds of other activities. We kids were all taught how to folk and square dance here and in elementary school. I loved the weight and feel of my petticoats spinning around me and brushing against my legs. Of course, at home Mutti played the piano and sometimes Papa played the accordion, but mostly Papa sang. He sang songs like 'The Tennessee Waltz' or children's songs in all sorts of languages, but mostly what he was known for, were his Mexican and Spanish love songs. The housewives around us would throw open their windows to hear him.

Sometimes, as they hung out their wash, they would sigh to me. 'You're such a lucky child! Your father has such a lovely voice.'

On one sunny warm day I ran up to him in the garden and asked, 'Papa? Why are you always singing?'

He answered with a chuckle, 'Oh, I do not even sing as much as my Mama used to. Sometimes I think she sang more then she talked!'

This made me giggle. Papa took off his straw cowboy hat wiped his brow and continued. 'I too, as a little boy, asked her why she sang so much, and she said, "It is because there is a lot to sing about."' Papa chuckled again. 'Of course, she was right.'

'Do you think we could sing about everything?' I asked. 'Like they do in the movies sometimes?'

Papa thought about it a minute, then replied, 'I don't see why not. Think about it, we sing songs of love but also of great battles in war or tell poems or stories about them, which to me is a kind of singing too. We sing songs to God. We sing songs about our country. We sing everything from Happy Birthday to our tragedies.'

'What are tragedies?' I asked.

'They are songs, poetry and stories that have sad endings.' Papa walked over to our silver maple tree and leaned against it.

I frowned slightly. 'Why would anyone want to listen to a story or song with a sad ending?'

Papa let out a big sigh. 'Because we must also sing songs that are true. Life can be hard and sad as well as happy. Bad things happen just like they did to Jesus on the cross and to Romeo and Juliet.'

'I know Jesus died on the cross, but who are Romeo and Juliet?'

'It is a famous story of two young people in love. In the story they died soon after they married.'

'Jesus died a long time ago too, so maybe we don't have to have so many tragedies now,' I responded, brightening at the thought.

'No, my sweet. Sad to say but happiness and tragedies are all part of the deal here on earth. When I was a boy, I was witness to such a moment. I was around your age, somewhere around ten. I was playing in a small park, across the street from our ice-cream shop downtown, where the kids of all ages would go after school. It was a time when rules were very strict, especially for the young. If you wanted to bend rules you waited until you were grown up enough and you could leave town and to go to the big city. Blacks, Mexicans and Whites did not go out with each other or even think to marry.

'Anyway, there was this girl. Her father was a very rich man and she was beautiful, with very white skin and black hair. Some said she had a Mexican grandmother on her mother's side, but she was treated as white, since her father had much money. Boys and girls in those days either went to separate schools or sat at different sides of the classroom. If there were a few Blacks, or poor kids from wherever it was, OK, as long as they caused no trouble and kept their mouths shut. So, one day this pretty girl comes out of the ice cream shop with her two friends and this black boy, who is in her class, walks up to her and asks her if she could tell him what the homework was that day, because he had to help his father at home and missed class. She wrote it down on a piece of paper for him and he said thank you and left. Many people saw that exchange, from inside the shop, or those who were passing by or, like I did, from across the street in the park. That next morning that boy was found hung from a tree in the very park I had been playing in, with the note pinned to his chest. The poor girl nearly went crazy and was sent to family back east for a long time. I overheard this from the adults around me.'

'They killed him!' I gasped. 'Did they catch who did it?'

'No, though everyone knew why it was done. Black boys do not talk to white girls let alone ask things from them. That is how it was then,' Papa said flatly, staring at the ground. 'It is things like this that are written about in stories, poetry and songs to remind people of how tragic life can be, especially for the innocent.'

We stood silent for a moment till I asked, 'Black people sing songs to Jesus, right?'

'Yes.' Papa nodded.

'And Mexican people sing to Jesus in their fancy castle-like churches and white people sing hymns in their churches?'

'That is right. They are singing about God and Jesus, but they are not all singing the same type of song. Every church is different.'

'But, Papa! We may all look different and sound different, but it IS all the same song! We are all singing our stories and feelings about God. Everyone all over the world sings about life, God, Jesus and so many songs about love. Why don't they see that? We are all singing the same songs about the same things, all over the world!'

'Ah,' he chuckled, 'I see now what you mean, little one. Do you know that some say that, when God made the world with his word, he then sang all living things to life? This is called by some *the song of all songs* and this was the first breath of life.'

'Why don't we all sing that song, Papa?'

Papa looked up to the sky a moment before speaking. 'I think because you first have to have the heart and mind to hear it and that takes hard work. Most people are too lazy to work that hard. God has been left waiting a long time for people to not be so selfish, so they can even hear let alone learn it.'

'I hope to hear and learn it sometime, Papa.'

'Me too,' Papa said. He flashed a big smile and put his hat back on. 'But for now, let us sing a song of donkeys while we pick tomatoes.'

I love that donkey song to this day.

My Papa and I cutting lilacs at the same spot we had that conversation so long ago. Mutti passed on three years ago and he is not far behind, but when we sing together the light still shines in his eyes to bring a moment of comfort and joy to my sister and me.

Gateways

The written word can flash off the page and jump into our hearts. I remember my nervous excitement at the first competition for our tenth-grade dramatic reading and debate team. We were asked to present prose or poetry. My desire was to do something with written images that really spoke to me. My eyes fell on one of my favorite albums by Simon and Garfunkel and the song *The Sound of Silence* leapt to mind. This became my poem. I will never forget the looks on the judges' faces as I solemnly read the lyric poem. As soon as I finished, a debate ensued among the judges as to whether my choice was allowable, in other words were lyrics really poetry? Sagely, it was agreed that the piece was indeed poetry. This was not the first time that I had raised eyebrows regarding my choices with poetry.

I must have been around twelve years old when our teacher wrote Goat, Boat, Float, Moat on the blackboard. She looked us over wearily - it had already been a hard week with summer break only a week away.

'This week, as part of English, we will be looking at rhyming in poetry,' she informed us. 'Yesterday, we spoke of a type of poetry called limericks, so today you will use these words to create your own limerick.'

I looked at the words on the blackboard with welling horror. My hand shot up almost of its own accord.

'Yes, Cornelia?' said my teacher, casting a baleful eye my way.

'Would it be all right, ahmm... please let it be all right for me to do this limerick using any words that rhyme, no goats and boats please?' I asked, meekly pleading a little at the end of my request.

The teacher leaned over her desk, gripping its sides, and peered above her wing-tipped glasses at me.

'I tell you what, *little Miss I have to be different,* I will make you a deal. You can do the assignment like everyone else, OR you can write what you want but, if I do not like it, you will get an I for incomplete. It's your choice.'

Floating boats with goats danced like sugar plums through my head. The thought of playing it safe was somehow unthinkable.

'I will write my own poem,' I answered quietly.

The classroom instantly fell into three camps. There were the few whose eyes flashed with a brief light and the hope that somehow, I could pull it off. There were more that thought I had lost my mind, and just as many that could not hide their wolfish grins at what would surely be my impending fall. If that was the case, it would give fodder for torturous teasing for the next week until summer break. Determined and inspired, I put pencil to paper. After about fifteen minutes the teacher started to call out students' names. She sat stone-like at her desk, with her eyes closed, as students read out their brave efforts. After about twelve rounds of floating goats in boats or moats, she calmly, but somewhat icily, said my name. I stood up and read:

> *There was a girl that could smile,*
> *She also could walk a mile,*
> *But two she couldn't,*
> *She just wouldn't do it,*
> *So, she sat down to rest for a while.*

You could hear a pen drop in the room. I was standing there, transfixed and, in what seemed like an eternity, we watched the teacher's face twitch until a scary, huge grin broke across it.

'This is what I was hoping to hear!' she beamed. 'What gave you this idea, Cornelia?'

'I... I don't know. It just came to me,' I stammered.

'Ahh… so, here we also have an example of being inspired by the poet's muse, classroom,' she announced grandly, then continued by asking, 'Besides the romantic notion of a muse, what else inspires us?'

'Fear!' called out the smart-ass kid in the class.

'Yes.' She nodded. 'Fear can be very inspirational. So, can revulsion.' She paused, chalk in hand and inquired of me, 'Do you have a fear or revulsion of goats, Cornelia?'

'No… I just found goats and boats too silly for me,' I answered truthfully.

'Limericks, by their very nature, are supposed to be somewhat silly but, be that as it may, what you were really confronting was a battle against mediocrity!' the teacher announced. With an elegant hand drew the word on the blackboard.

By this time, I was sitting down, and we were all somewhat open-mouthed that my little poem, a limerick at that, was causing our stoned-face teacher to wax profoundly over our heads.

'Mediocrity! To be common, to be like everyone else and not attempt to excel,' the teacher explained to the class as she walked over to my desk. She leaned down toward me to say, 'You will get your grade, Cornelia, but remember doing things your own way does not always work out so well.' She bent her head, looked down at me over her glasses and intoned, 'So, pick your battles wisely.'

I somehow managed to smile a little and murmured thank you. Yet, in the back of my mind I understood that something important had just happened, even though I could not fully grasp it all. What I did realize, despite what seemed like her ominous warning to me, was that I really did like her as a teacher, and I deeply regretted accidentally hitting her in the face with a basketball the week before.

Here I am around twelve and my sister around six, with Mutti

The years pass. Now I write another poem:

Threshold

The mythical puzzle
The mystical cup
The banquet of life
I must sup.
The labyrinthine doorway
The sacred sacrifice
The dance at the threshold
I must survive.

How did I come from my simple childhood rhyme that, no doubt, was surely describing a part of myself, to create this poem of spiritual determination and depth?

Perhaps on the surface one could say; *yes, Cornelia's teacher was right about her childhood poem. Here are her beginnings that show her future tendencies, born out of her distaste for the simple, for being given boundaries, rules to follow, or perhaps being forced to be on the same level as everyone else.*

There may be some truth to these ideas; I was after all, a child at the time. Yet, I think that there may be something more at play. Something more than the fear of a bad grade, or the dreaded mediocrity that so sounded like some awful disease to my young ears, but something subtler and more deeply human, reflecting ultimately our natural connection to the universe of the spirit that is poetry's conduit.

The day before our poetry readings our teacher had read children's poems and limericks by Lewis Carroll and Edward Lear to us. We, especially I, were transported by the rhyme. My mind's eye clearly saw the birds in a man's beard, while my fledgling consciousness was being, dare I say, 'goosed' into grasping the concept of the ironic, the poignant and the possibility of the mastery of sheer silliness. When those poems made me laugh, it was like my mind or spirit embraced some inner secret of human nature and it was beautiful. After that, the ingenuous or the trite could not compare; something deep inside me could not mock this art form with the inane or the ridiculously simplistic. I had to step up to the plate and give my best effort to the spirit of poetry that had now been awakened in me.

The Laws of Science, Poetry and Golf

Our middle school was a beautiful old building that was, in its time, the best of American educational architecture. It contained spacious classrooms and many features and amenities, such as its own swimming pool. But what made me feel that I had arrived at the doorway leading to adulthood was our science department. Mr. Fredricks, our science and physics teacher, was not a geek or nerd in any sense of the word. He was very handsome in the manly way that invoked instant respect from the boys and shy awe from most of the girls. The minute you walked into his classroom, it demanded respect, from its Roman colosseum-like seating that tiered up one half of the room, to the huge, long blackboard on the other. Mr. Fredricks slowly paced in front of this board with deliberate steps as he shot out questions or drew thereon the mysterious symbols and mathematical formulas that explained the secrets of our universe. It was all very impressive.

My friend Mary was in this class with me and we loved everything about it. Mr. Fredricks made a point to sit us on each side of the classroom, not only to keep us from whispering or giggling, but as he remarked one day, 'You girls are not always right but at least you are thinking! You also ask good questions, so if I put you on the opposite sides of the room maybe it will get everyone else in the room thinking too!'

The smartest boy in the room snickered. He was a wiz at everything, but especially so with math and science. Since he was usually a very quiet type, this boy was quite horrified when Mr. Fredricks' booming voice was directed at him and filled the room. 'Yes! We are very well aware of the fact that you are most likely the smartest kid in the room, but you never say anything, so what good are you!?'

The poor kid turned deep red.

'Now!' Mr. Fredricks said, regaining his good humor, 'what is wonderful about science classes is that you get to do cool stuff!' He beamed. 'I am now going to assign you lab seats.'

We dutifully walked into a large room with rows of kitchen-like counters. Our names were called off and, to my surprise and pleasure, Mary was my partner. Experimental stations were already set up on the counters. Our first experiment had to do with magnetism. The point of which was that, when one runs a current through two small metal strips, the strips would press together or fall apart depending if the current was on or off. A very simple experiment. We were then directed to add a magnet later to change the course of the results later.

'Mary,' I whispered, 'I don't think this will turn out as he expects.'

'Why not, hon?' she chuckled. 'It's a very simple law of physics, not even you can mess that up. Yet... hmm.' She paused, humming very softly with one eye closed and apparently rethinking her comment.

'OK,' instructed Mr. Fredricks, 'One of you will plug in underneath your lab counter, while the other should immediately observe that the metal strips, which are widely apart not clasped together, will immediately hug together.'

I plugged in and immediately heard Mary say, 'Oh dear, I see what you mean.'

I slowly raised my head over the counter and eyed the metal tabs still apart. I unplugged, and they hugged together.

'Check the plugs!' I whispered desperately. Which we did and of course nothing changed.

Then the teacher's voice boomed across the large room,

'Now, flip your switches on the counter and observe the tabs flatten together tightly.'

'Mary, you flip the switch!' I pleaded.

'No. By all means, Cornelia, I would not dream of interfering with you and the laws of science.' She grinned.

'Are you girls having a problem of some kind?' inquired Mr. Fredricks from across the room.

I was sinking in my shoes and stammered out. 'For some strange reason, it is working backwards.'

Mr. Fredricks drew himself up to his full height and adjusted his belt a touch, making me picture him, in my mind, wearing a big cowboy hat and about to duel with the stuff and nonsense of two barely teenage girls.

He strode over to us and said, 'Impossible. That would go against the laws of nature and science.'

I pointed to the little strips.

He glared at them as one might at an unruly child before lowering his face toward me and saying, 'Now, you are smart girls so are you playing a little trick or joke on me, hmmm?'

Mary, in a very no-nonsense tone, quickly said; 'Now when would we have had the time to do that, especially when we had no idea what was going to happen in class today?'

'That is true but not impossible. I will find out the truth of this.' He proceeded to re-plug the main plug as the rest of the class drew closer.

My cheeks felt burning hot. They were most likely bright red, which embarrassed me all the more. I feared it made me look guilty, or silly at the very least. But the teacher's action brought the same results.

He hmphed and flipped the switch and the results were still backwards. He unplugged the whole experiment and went over every connection, rewiring and re-plugging everything. Then he looked up to the class and asked, 'I can safely assume this has not happened to anyone else?'

The class shook their heads, or muttered no.

'Very good, then. There is nothing wrong with this station or experiment. Cornelia, plug in again...'

'Oh, please let Mary have a turn,' I half suggested and half pleaded.

'Cornelia, your presence cannot affect the laws of physics and science. Please plug in,' Mr. Fredricks said again.

Resigned, I plugged in and then stood with everyone else as our little lab experiment still defied all of us and the laws of science. The teacher flicked the switch on and off to no avail, as the little strips seemed determined to behave backwards.

'Impossible!' he muttered between clenched teeth. Then with a great sigh he looked at me and asked, 'Do you have any theory or possible explanation for this?'

'I think it's because of my father,' I offered meekly.

'How could your father have anything to do with this?' he glowered.

'Well, for one thing, he can't wear a watch of any kind for very long because they all stop on him.'

'Bad choice of watches, perhaps?' Mr. Fredricks offered.

'Lights will flicker, or go on and off, even street lights sometimes. Other odd things will happen once in a while too. My mother says it's because Papa has strong feelings and gives off a strong energy.'

'Well, that is nonsense.'

'Why so?' challenged Mary. 'Did you not say our brain is a type of electric chemistry and that we all have energy that runs through us?'

The poor man put his hands on his hips and said, 'I have to think about this. Class dismissed.'

The next day I was a little late to class, so I happened to be the last one in. I wondered what Mr. Fredricks had come up with. Maybe he would just drop the whole thing, which

I did not think was likely, but I still hoped.

He smiled at me as I walked in and called out in a friendly voice, 'Cornelia, will you flip on the switch on the far right for our overhead lights.'

'Sure.' I flashed back a big smile and flipped the switch.

The lights overhead in the room brightened then dimmed, causing all of us to look up, then in the lab room next door, we heard a loud popping sound like a little explosion. All the kids turned their heads towards the open lab door. More loud pops and fizzles went off as lab stations exploded, one right after the other. My mouth dropped open. Mr. Fredricks and I stared at each other in mute horror.

As the last pop sounded, he said in a shocked voice, 'I worked six hours last night setting that up...Why, why of all people did you have to be the last one in'?

'Karma!' called out one of the hippie boys.

'Serendipity!' challenged the smart kid.

'Fate,' added Mary with a tone of both amusement and pride in her voice.

I started to melt. 'Oh, please, you know that I would never... I am so sorry...You told me to do it... You told me...' I was nearly in tears.

Mr. Fredricks visibly pulled himself together. 'Cornelia, please sit down. This certainly was not your fault. I must have overloaded the system.'

After class, Mary and Mr. Fredricks had their heads together for a few minutes.

When she joined, me she smiled and said, 'He is still thinking.'

'Great...' I said, then thought to myself, *I can't wait for tomorrow.*

The next day was blissfully uneventful until the end of class when Mr. Fredricks called Mary and me over to his desk and handed us two envelopes.

'Please give those to either or both of your parents and have them sign them and bring them back to me tomorrow or no later than Friday,' he instructed.

'What is this?' I asked

'This is an invitation for you and Mary to go golfing with me,' he grinned.

I was shocked. Never would I have guessed at an invitation of any kind coming from Mr. Fredricks, let alone to go golfing. I had never even played the game and told him so. No need to worry he reassured me. Mary had played before and he and Mary would teach me. He then shooed us out of the door.

Mary and I began to walk home by the way of the railroad tracks. Mary, my other good friend Betty and I all loved to walk, or even run, for as long as we could on the rails until we tired or slipped off. The tracks were seldom used, so it was a fairly safe game.

'Mary, are you a part of this? I mean what is this all about?' I prodded.

'It is going to be an experiment!' Mary was grinning from ear to ear. 'And we, *especially you,* are a part of it.'

'What does this have to do with golf?' I was very confused.

'Apparently, everything,' laughed Mary.

It was a lovely day with only a hint of a gentle breeze. I had never been on a golf course before and I was very impressed with the swirling flattened grass going, as far as I could see, over gentle hills and little oases scattered about. Mary and Mr. Fredricks were already engaged in lively discussion.

'Golf is a kind of perfection.' He beamed, taking in a big lungful of fresh air. 'Here, in this lovely peaceful setting, humans exercise both the body and the mind. First the body by walking, second by controlled and disciplined muscle movements and then the mind by applying sound scientific laws. The counterbalance of variables is pure poetry.'

'How do you figure that?' I asked.

Mr. Fredricks took another deep breath and adjusted his belt a bit. 'First of all, the purpose of the game is to get your ball into the holes at the bottom of the flag poles in as few a number of strokes as you can. The winner is the one with the lowest score not the highest.'

'Can you do it in one hit if you are good enough?' I asked.

'That is called a hole in one,' he said, 'and is almost impossible, but once in a great while the impossible comes into play and this is where the poetry comes in. It is a part of the romance of the game.'

I was given a brief lecture on the different golf clubs and the laws of inertia and kinetic energy, as well as on inner visual geometry to try and figure out the best angles. This was in addition to the rules of the game I had to take in, and all the walking. My head was spinning trying to absorb it all.

'How can you even enjoy the game when you have all this hard thinking to do?' I complained a little. 'I would rather just give it my best shot by my best instincts and see what happens.'

Mr. Fredricks smiled broadly. 'That is what I thought you might feel. Have you noticed how Mary's shots have improved as she's modified her posture and put more thought into what she's doing? Just like poetry. Sure, you can be inspired and have the intent of putting that inspiration to paper, but for it to leap from the page in a truly professional manner one must put some discipline into it with meter, line, rhyme and rhythm.'

'I don't think that this is the way Cornelia works most of the time,' stated Mary, getting off a nice far shot.

Mr. Fredricks nodded approval at her shot but replied,

'Nonsense, the whole cosmos lives by laws, and there is a rare mutation now and then to allow change for some sensible reason or another and this is how science and nature planned it.' He walked now with a little bounce in his step. 'Nature is a part of science, not above it.'

'But there are many influences in this world, Mr. Fredricks. Like you said, the wind is only one of them. What about the energies inside us and around us?' I piped up bravely.

'So, by that you must mean God is a part of energy, I suppose. I am sure many a prayer and curse have been said upon these fields and that takes energy too.' Mr. Fredrick's chuckled. 'Pick a club, Cornelia. Stand in place and hit that ball as far as you can towards the field below. Try and get it as close as you can get to the flag. As you stand there, think of what laws, rules and skills will most help you to attain your goal.'

I went to the bag and made my pick. I felt the weight of the club in my hand as Mr. Fredricks kindly teed my ball. My biggest concern was hitting the ground and not having what he called 'a good follow through'. Not managing to hit the ball at all would be the ultimate humiliation. We were up on a hill and there were puffs of wind coming from the left to right. I thought I would hit a little to the left so that the wind would push the ball back towards the middle of the field. If I hit it strongly enough, it would hopefully hit the green not too far from the hole. I closed my eyes for a second and yes, I did think that if there were any Spirits or Angels around that would like to help me, even just for fun, I would certainly appreciate it. I took a deep breath, held it and took my shot.

There was that wonderful THWACK sound as the ball sailed through the air like a tiny white cannon ball, heading straight for the flag pole. We watched as it hit the pole square on and bunny-hopped right next to the hole. The look on Mr. Fredricks' face was priceless and a little scary, especially when he started to jump up and down throwing his clubs hither and yon.

Mary came and put her arm around me. 'Don't worry,' she soothed, 'he'll calm down in a moment.'

After walking back and forth for a while, Mr. Fredricks picked up both his and Mary's clubs, pointed one at me and asked firmly, 'You have never played before?'

'No, I have not. This is my first time,' I replied resolutely.

He grabbed my club and placed it with all the others in the big bag with wheels. 'Yet, Mary plays, and you are good friends?'

'My parents don't have the money for golf.' I sighed.

He humphed and we headed to my brave little ball, which was sitting like an expectant pup right by the flag. Mr. Fredricks pulled out the flag, handed me a different club and told me to punt it in, which I did. He stared down into the hole with such sorrow it gave me an eerie feeling, as if we were at some graveside mourning my poor, valiant little ball.

'Well, then,' Mary broke the silence, 'I guess part of the lesson is that beginners' luck is somehow tied to the laws of mutation or maybe somehow to poetry.'

Mr. Fredricks glowered sourly my way 'And what do you think the other part is, Cornelia?'

'Perhaps that if the laws of science and nature are set-in motion by forces we do not always understand, they can change the rules a little whenever they feel like it.'

'Great, just great,' muttered Mr. Fredricks. 'Let's get something to eat.'

Mary and I were soon munching hungrily on hamburgers at the golf club while Mr. Fredricks thoughtfully sipped a small beer his food untouched.

Poetry Becomes Lyric

By the ages of sixteen and seventeen, a new awakening guided my future interests and opened my heart to the written word, and the exploration of all things creative, in a whole new way. I now read the words in my hymnal book in church as poetry and was amazed at the storytelling power of those songs when I read them aloud. Hymns like *The Old Rugged Cross* and *Amazing Grace* now made me even more curious about their history. I found out, to my shock, that *The Old Rugged Cross* had been written in my hometown of Albion, Michigan. Also, that there was quite a story behind the song *Amazing Grace* – so much so, that it was later told in a movie of that same name. It also seemed to me that the melodies lifted this kind of poetry to another level, as if entreating and drawing up the person to follow the words and notes to the very doors of heaven. These were very heady and dizzying thoughts for a young teen. I thought of old beloved nursery rhymes and stories, in which both children and adults were taught the ways of virtue. I thought of great inspiring works of pagan art and writings, as well as the breath-taking beauty of the old cathedrals and the mesmerizing chants of their choirs. It seemed that adulthood would hold the answers to so many mysteries and I was so looking forward to getting there.

This heightened awareness of the power of words also broadened my taste in music; from the happy-go-lucky Monkees, The Beatles and The Dave Clark Five to Steven Stills, Carol King, Buffy St. Marie, Leonard Cohen and even Led Zeppelin. All these began to trickle onto the play list of our little town's radio station. I began to wonder why certain melodies and words could so easily catch my ear and deeply move my young heart. Was it the strong emotive words coupled with the drama of music? My generation had embraced it all with open arms, all the words and sounds that could range from the sublime to the thunderous.

At the time of The Beatles and The Monkees, I was still barely a teen. I remember my carefree days playing in my girlfriend's basement. There, we played The Game of Life, during which my friend laughed at me every time for being so appalled that one could sell anything, even one's own children, to win the game.

'It's OK,' my girl-friend pronounced soothingly, 'It's just a game.' This – while giggling at my discomfort.

We were such busy little bees in her basement, also playing endless rounds of Monopoly, Battleship, Checkers and Twister. On dark, rainy Fall nights, we broke out the Ouija board in an effort to find the names of our future husbands. We would hold our breath and deeply hope that the spirit world would talk to us or, at least let itself be known by the board floating off our laps or something equally dramatic and ghostly. Nothing quite so phenomenal happened, other than once, when the heart-shaped planchette went flying off the table while our hands were barely on it. This caused us to squeal like frightened little piglets. We retrieved the reluctant planchette, now missing its little bronze pointer nail, and after a thorough but fruitless search for the nail, we prudently returned the Ouija board to its box and said box back to the closet.

Looking back now, it seems that it was in the blink of an eye that board games were replaced by learning to dance and how we should do our hair. The basement was our lair until the day after I came home from a short vacation. I was around fifteen or sixteen. That day I found my friend languishing in her bedroom, with no desire to head for the sanctuary of our basement cave. At first, she would not share with me what had made her so pensive and blue, until finally she confessed she was in the throes of her first serious crush. I suggested we go to the basement and play some music and dance.

'I don't listen to that kid stuff anymore. I listen to this.' She pointed to some albums lying on the windowsill. On top was this open album with a shocking yet wonderful scene: an elven beauty, naked and standing boldly out on the rocks facing towards a churning sea, her long blond hair whipping in the ocean winds, with the greens and blues of nature all around her. The scene quite took the breath out of my modest teen frame.

'Her name is Joni Mitchell. She is so deep and so free.' said my friend worshipfully.

I felt oddly pulled in two like a sheet of torn paper. The dutiful, innocent Lutheran girl was saying, '*HEY! We are not supposed to look at naked people!*' Yet, there was this other feeling that welled up from somewhere deep inside me, just as strongly and it was: '*WOW! This picture is beautiful, period.*' It was not just the lovely woman with her blond hair flying in the wind and spray. It was everything in the picture that just stopped me in my tracks and made some kind of light turn on inside of me.

'Oh, come on!' admonished my friend, shaking me out of my frozen stare. 'Don't be a prude. Think of all the naked statues around the world and all the famous naked paintings. They are art and so is this.'

'I am not a prude! I was just surprised, that's all,' I said, defending myself. 'It is such a pretty picture.'

'She is *so* brave. Just listen to her sing!' For the first time since I'd arrived, a smile broke through on my friend's face. She hurried to her record player and turned it on.

Joni's ethereal voice and lilting melodies filled the room as I continued to gaze at the album cover and its other pictures. I glanced at the lyrics that were printed there while taking in this new sound.

'She's a Goddess, isn't she?' stated my friend.

The light was turning golden as it came through the window and I knew I had to head home.

'Glad you were home,' I said. 'Nice to see you for a bit. See you later.' I called out brightly as I bounced down the stairs. Inside I felt a little nervous for I knew something had somehow changed…

My mother was in the kitchen as I popped in. 'I need to ask you something,' I burst out to her.

'Sure, go right ahead,' she offered

'Well, on many of your classical record albums there are pictures of naked people.'

'Yes… Usually statues or paintings, but yes, there are,' she confirmed.

'Why?' I asked flatly.

She dried her hands and chose her words carefully.

'In the Bible, and in other classical writings, it was said that the human body is a reflection of God's image. So, like all creation, it is perfect and beautiful when it's presented as something sacred.'

'Oh, OK, that makes sense.' Then I grinned mischievously and asked, 'So, why are people so uptight about naked pictures now?' I was – maybe just a wee bit – coy in my tone.

One eyebrow shot up as she eyed me. 'Remember, I said *presented as something sacred.*'

'So, you do mean sacred like in godly or godlike?'

'Not quite always having to do with God directly; it can also be about nature, as in what is healthy, natural and sacred in nature. This often inspires poetry. There is a big difference between a girl or women lying naked next to a river or lake, maybe about to take her bath, or even a woman modeling for an artist, then a woman who presents her bosom like a tray of cookies.'

She grabbed a cookie tray, slipped it under her ample breasts and leaned forward making a funny smoochie face.

'Mutti!' I cried out. I was almost on the floor with laughter.

'What's going on in there?' boomed my father from the living room where he was watching the news of the day.

'Oh, nothing,' said my mother with a wink as she slipped the tray back into its place.

I was still giggling as I ran upstairs to wash up for supper.

That night I lay in bed awake, thinking about the day. I had been so eager to come home from our little trip, so that I could go back to being with my friend. Yet, after only a few short days, everything seemed completely different. The album's photos and Joni's music kept coming to mind. She must be very brave, I thought, and have a lot of trust that most people would see her picture as art and as something natural and beautiful, as my friend and I did. I was sure some others would think of it as a cheap or crass ploy to sell records. Then it hit me somehow that the picture was the result of what Joni Mitchell knew and felt to be true inside herself; that was why she could be so daring. It was a statement saying: *this is who I am and how I feel*. How she got there must be in her words in the songs. My friend had told me that Joni Mitchell's lyrics were pure poetry. I vowed to pay more attention to the words the next time I went to her house. I yawned, cuddled my stuffed animals and drifted to sleep, still unaware that childhood was very quickly slipping away from me.

Almost Grown in Michigan

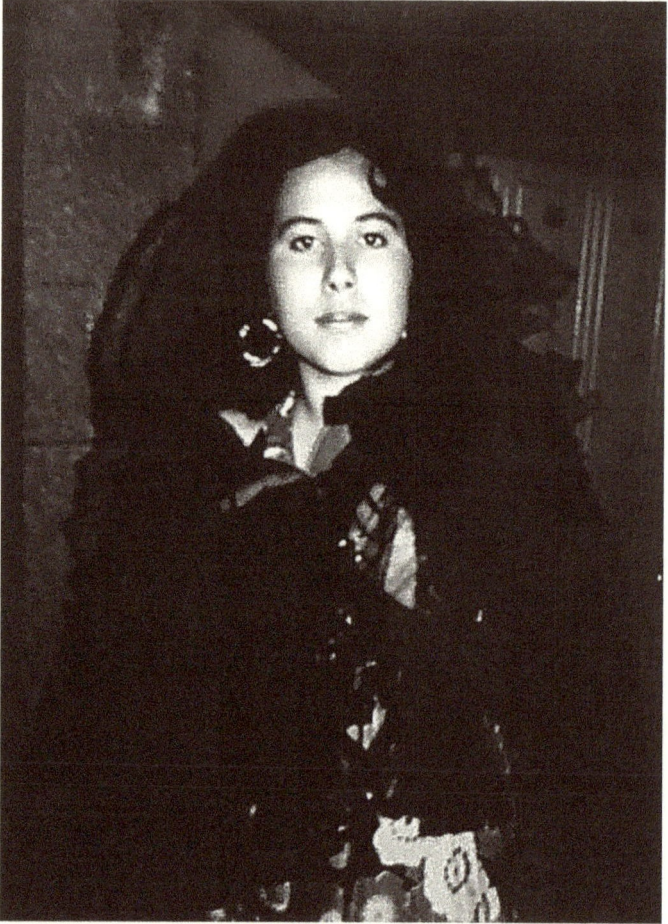

My theater days at seventeen

My next years were filled with the life of a teenager in small town America. The lovely lazy days of dreaming about romances we might have and trying to figure out the little dramas and turmoils of the day, as we all struggled with identity. It was the Seventies. The world was in the middle of a new birth, rethinking its possibilities and philosophy along with the coming wave of new technology that would sweep us into the future. What I did not know then was that the coming years would both caress and pound humanity like a growing pulse. This pulse filled all of us with hope and fear for the future of our earth. Yet, for the daring of mind and spirit, it was both a time of chaos and great creativity.

My first wave of change carried me from carefree days with Betty, exploring on our bikes and riding her pony Lucky, to embarking on those daring adventures of mind and spirit speaking deeply about everything from boys to magic. I also spent more time with my immediate neighbors; Mary B, Janet. Soon many of us were doing both community and high school musicals. My heart smiles and fills with pride at the daring of us kids. Our high school stage had not been used very much, but with the help of an understanding janitor we managed to sneak in and build the whole stage set for *Lil' Abner*. We sold tickets and I presented the whole project to our astonished Principal. Fortunately, he was pleased with our rebel clandestine musical and our production was a hit. Soon, my sister and I were involved at all levels from drama to musicals. We raised our community's eyebrows by casting parts through best audition and fit. With the encouragement of our high-school drama teacher, whose last name was, ironically, Hamlet, we produced the play *Flowers for Algernon*. We had a totally mixed-race cast, even in the family parts, with the intent that it not be about race at all, just the telling of the story. It was a proud moment when people told us that they became so mesmerized by the story and the acting, that the color of the actors seemed to disappear, even at the moment of the mixed-race kiss, and this was a surprise to them also.

Looking back, we were such brave and creative kids, from our choices of productions to forming the

'Ecumenical Choir' bringing kids from different denominations together to sing. Martha, Judy and Paula all played guitar and inspired me to learn to play myself. We dove into *Bye Bye Birdie*, *The Grinch that Stole Christmas* and *Charlie Brown*. Then my ultimate theatre dream came true when I was cast as Gypsy Rose Lee in the play *Gypsy*. As the old song says: 'Those were the days, my friend.'

Somehow, in the middle of the whirlwind of high school musicals and plays, Betty and I managed to volunteer with other kids from our high school for social youth work with the local Methodist church. We travelled to the South Carolina Islands, where the black people there speak a language called Gallah, also called Sea Creole and Geechee – this is a Creole language spoken by the Gullah people. These people carry the ways and language of their African past, mixed with Native American, French and a little Scot/Irish. It was like stepping into a different world. We helped repair very old houses and finished painting a new one with the most amazing shade of blinding green chartreuse. In the bright Carolina sun, that house became the marker point to all directions on the island for years to come.

The following year, this same group went to work with Native Americans in Oklahoma. Here we helped fix an old church and were witness to how the natives struggled with racism nearly every day. They fought for their way of life continually, even while seamlessly mixing the Christian world with their own spiritual culture.

My eyes were opened so much from these journeys. To this day I remember the black girl on St Johns Island, who braided my hair as we spoke of so many things as girls do. When we sadly sad good-bye, she told an incredulous me that I was the first white girl she had ever spoken to as a friend. She had lived her whole life on the island, only going to Charlton to help her mother clean houses, and she was not allowed to address white people. A black girl was only to speak when spoken to.

In Oklahoma I spoke with Native American kids who were finally allowed to come home from the boarding schools they had been forced to attend. Betty and I, along with two boys, came under attack in downtown Bristol from a grown man and his friends at a pool hall because we dared to speak to "his" Indian boy who was the pool cue holder. Thankfully Betty and I were fast and very load screamers, and we were rescued by the adults in our group.

What caught my ear as well as my eye in both these trips was the singing and rhythms of both the Gallah people in St Johns and the Native people in Oklahoma. In church, they all sang and beat the rhythm with their feet or drums and it was deeply moving to see and feel. I came to realize I lived in an exciting time of change, but that the need for this change grew out of a deep well of suffering and challenge for so many people. Though there has been progress in the last forty-five years there is still so much that needs to be done for the sake of the people and the land we live on.

My last jump into a different and unknown world before college was also an eye-opening experience: I worked as a camp counsellor, for developmentally challenged kids of all kinds, both physically and mentally, in a Christian camp in the hills of upper New York State. I learned that music and story-telling was a balm to the soul for these children. I also learned that courage and wisdom can come in all kinds of packages. Of course, I knew about children born without arms or legs or who had harelips, but I was not prepared at all for what confronted me with a sweet smile when I walked into her cabin. I had been told she was eleven. This child had the prettiest face that held all the promise of growing into a stunningly-beautiful woman. Her deep, soulful large blue eyes were framed by the longest, shiny brilliant yellow/white platinum hair I had ever seen. But this angelic face rested upon a short neck, and her shoulders were much too small. She had one normal arm, yet the other arm and hand were so badly crippled as to be almost totally useless. All this sat on about six inches of a truck-like stump. She was about eighteen inches tall.

My shock was apparent.

'Come, sit by me,' she said. 'Let's talk it out and get it all out of the way.' She spoke in the most comforting tone. 'I know I'm a shock because people like me don't usually live after being born.'

I sat down in front of her, barely able to find the words to speak hello and tell her my name.

She pushed a coloring book and some crayons at me and then started to tell me about herself. 'My parents are good kind Christian people and neither they nor the doctors know why I way born this way. I feel that this is what God wanted.'

'Why would God want such a thing?' I could not help but blurt out. 'It seems so cruel and unfair.'

'Yes,' she said totally unfazed. 'It does with my pretty face and hair on this broken body. Yet, on the other hand I am a miracle.' She smiled. 'I am a miracle every day I'm alive, and I have my gifts and I think I know why.'

'Why?' I asked her honestly.

'For one, I think that my pretty face and hair is a gift for me so that I too can be a little vain,' she giggled. 'For two I think someone like me forces people to consider that they are speaking to a soul and spirit inside this deformed body and by having only my face to focus on they have to pay attention to my words.'

I could not help but laugh. 'It's amazing you can feel this way. They told me when they assigned me to you that you are eleven.

'Oh yes, that reminds me,' she added. 'I'm smart too!

Smarter than most people, so I could grow up fast and do my job, because no one knows how long my normal-sized heart can grow and live in this tiny space.'

My eyes flew wide open, once again horrified.

She reached out to me with her good hand. 'Don't worry, I am happy, not in pain. I'm at peace with whatever happens. When I die, I'll have a spirit body and if there is such a thing as being born again here, I will ask God for a different assignment.' She winked. 'Now that I have told you everything, I hear you are going to take me swimming, so let's now talk about that.'

I was so humbled by these kids and that summer put in perspective that, no matter what hardships or challenges I had faced in life so far, I was still living a lucky life filled with more privilege then I realized.

After high school, I did a summer of what was called Summer Stock Theatre in Battle Creek, Michigan, before returning to begin my studies at Albion College. My first play there was *I Never Saw Another Butterfly*, in which I played a teenage girl who survives the death camp Auschwitz. My mother was in tears watching the play, the only time I ever saw her cry in public.

After my freshman year, at the still tender age of nineteen, I took a semester off to travel and adventure all around the country. This adventure gave me my first taste of San Francisco. It was 1974, and I was only there for about two weeks, with my two girlfriends Shirley and Maggie. The visit was only to have been for a few days, but our car had broken down. While there, Shirley and I stuffed dividend envelopes for PG&E to earn some extra money. This job was performed under armed guard, which made the workers, mostly girls and women, feel like prisoners rather than employees. However, it was the only way that my girlfriends and I could get our broken-down car fixed and be able to return home to Michigan.

It was there, during this time, that I met a lovely woman called Robin. She sang for change in the streets of China Town in San Francisco. One day she invited me to sing with her, which I did. She told me that she had been married to a well-known architect in Canada, but that he had not wanted her to play guitar or sing, so she'd left him and their beautiful home in Canada, to come to San Francisco and live like a modern gypsy. Robin spoke seriously with me about what it meant to be a woman who rules her own heart and future. She announced that the tools to truly finding oneself lay in poetry, art, dance, music, all of which is storytelling in its many forms. Robin also told me that, if I paid attention to others who are authentic and true to themselves, I would also find what is true and authentic in me, and that this was what I must share with the world.

More heady stuff for a young girl at the end of her teens and still on the edge of true womanhood. I remembered Robin's words, despite not comprehending fully their meaning and depth until much later.

I returned with Maggie to college in Michigan to study Philosophy, Psychology and Theater, while Shirley stayed in San Francisco, but Robin's words and the foghorns of the city never stopped calling to me. After I graduated college, I had a choice to go east and continue studying at the Moreno Institute of Psychodrama, or to return to San Francisco. I decided to return there, though at the time, in some ways, I so wished to make other plans. I was leaving behind family, love and the door to a good career. My spiritual, poetic and still innocent heart called me West.

Poetry and Magic in San Francisco

My friend Shirley and I had been looking for good Mexican food, maybe with some noontime Mariachi bands, in San Francisco's Mission District. We ended up at a little restaurant on the corner of Albion and Sixteenth streets. I was very amused to find an Albion anything here on the west coast, let alone a street in the Mission District with the same name as my Michigan hometown. The smells wafting out of this restaurant made my mouth water.

'This is the place that has great Chile Rellenos,' Shirley

pronounced as I followed her inside. Soon we were munching on some of the Mission's best Mexican food.

As we were eating, I observed an impressive looking woman entering the restaurant, apparently for a take-out lunch. She had an amazing shade of dark red hair, which lay just over her shoulders. Even though she was heavyset, she had a sexy kind of Valkyrie aura about her. I whispered to Shirley, 'Check out the woman with the amazing red hair.'

Shirley turned around and turned back quick, her big dark eyes wide and sparkling. 'Oh yes!' she whispered back, 'I have seen her around. She's a real witch like Starhawk – the woman who wrote the acclaimed book, *The Spiral Dance* – but not from the same group, I think.'

I laughed a little and whispered, 'Shirley, you are always saying how shy you are, but you know the most remarkable things about people.'

Shirley's cheeks turned a little rosy. 'I just pay attention and listen,' she mumbled into her cola.

The woman left with her lunch and Shirley headed back up to the Haight/Ashbury, while I returned to my new home, which was an artist co-op called Project One.

A few weeks later, I was in the same area exploring little second-hand shops and bookstores, when it occurred to me to go to and explore Albion Street. I had heard that it was lined with fragrant trees and that the houses there held lovely apartments. It was not that long a block, but it was its own little world, with the bustle and noise of Sixteenth and Mission strangely distant. The buildings were two to three stories high and not really like San Francisco's traditional Victorians, but more like brick brownstones with Victorian bay windows. Between the height of the buildings and the trees lining the street, it was cooler and darker than the glare just around the corner. I was about midway through the block when I recognized her, holding

Transpiration

a bag of groceries and reaching in the pocket of her long dress for her keys.

'Oh, hello,' I greeted her walking up. 'I saw you getting lunch at the corner restaurant a few weeks ago.'

She looked up at me and raised an eyebrow. 'You have a good memory, then.'

'My friend Shirley used to know Starhawk and she said that you are a witch as well, so I am curious now that I have run into you.'

She looked straight into my face with bright, light sea-green eyes, so I could not help but add, 'My mother has green eyes, but they are darker than yours like a moss green. I always wanted green eyes too.'

'And why is that?' she asked, narrowing hers slightly.

'I've been told that to have green eyes means you have a drop of fairy blood in you.'

For the first time, she smiled. A crooked smile, but it removed the suspicion from her face. 'That is old lore from way back. Would you like to come in for coffee or tea?'

'That would be lovely,' I responded.

She allowed me to take one of her bags and we went inside.

The air was cool in the large apartment and we were greeted by an unusually colored cat. The cat had an unusual name as well and was introduced as 'Varuka'. The cat trilled and pranced on delicate gray paws. Varuka was quite slender like a Siamese, but displayed very large olive-green eyes, with fur that was a patchwork of soft light grey, pale pinky orange and a darker blue grey.

We set the bags on the kitchen table and returned to a large living room with comfortable chairs. I was bid to sit down.

'My name is Margaret, by the way,' my hostess told me.

'Mine is Cornelia,' I offered back.

'That's an old Latin name. You don't hear it too often. Would you like a cool herbal tea or a warm one?'

'Whatever you're having,' I responded.

'I'm having some children's tea. It's naturally sweet and calming, a mother's boon.'

'Does that mean blessing or gift?' I asked with a furrowed brow, hoping I did not sound ignorant.

An honest throaty laugh escaped Margaret's lips. 'Well, one could suppose that it is a gift to the kid who is getting the tea, and not being punished for racing around like a crazed squirrel, and a blessing to the mom for calming her kid down.'

I chuckled with her. 'I have never heard of children's tea in Michigan, but my grandmother in Germany knows a lot about herbs and wild mushrooms and many other things.'

'Ah, a wonderful kind of grandmother to have. Mine chased a bear back into the woods with a broom for being at the front door uninvited.'

'That's amazing! I guess you could say we come from good stock.'

'Indeed. So… why are you curious about witchcraft?' she asked, getting to the point, as she poured some tea.

'I guess a part of it is what brought *you* to it? Were you born that way, or is being psychic being a witch? I'm not totally ignorant of these things, because of my family, but I feel I'm still a little confused. Like, if you are a witch, and have been born that way, why would people say you have to hate God or Jesus?'

'Sounds like you've been thinking about this a while.'

'I come from a creative, and somewhat psychically gifted family and have always seemed a little different, even to my friends. Yet, my family somehow fitted smoothly into the Christian church, no matter what else they might think or believe. But, for me....'

'No matter how hard you tried, no matter how sincere your heart, it was like trying to pound your square little head into a round hole,' Margaret interjected softly.

'Yes! That is exactly how it felt, and it was so

uncomfortable. I felt so foolish! Like I was failing at everything – being a good daughter, being a good person and even failing God.'

'So, how did you deal with all those feelings?' Margaret asked.

'I had a talk with God. I said to him: "Look God, you are supposed to know everything, and you made me the way I am. You are supposed to be a righteous God, which means you must be good and fair…"'

Margaret cleared her throat and interrupted, 'I must argue with that interpretation. You are not the only reasonable person to think or feel that way, but righteous actually means to be right as decreed by divine law. It is the shield all Christians stand behind that justifies anything they say or do for God or Jesus, because God is ever righteous, therefore ever right, as the Bible spells it out.'

'Well, then…' I let out a big breath. 'According to what I was taught, God knows my heart, so I can only assume he knew what I meant, or at least my intent.'

'That is very gracious and optimistic of you,' responded Margaret, somewhat dryly before she took a sip of her tea. 'Please continue.'

'I told God that I was going to explore his world and to please not play with me or allow me to be led astray by someone or something that is much smarter than me.'

Margaret jumped in again. 'You mean like Eve, almost a newborn babe, up against Lucifer, God's most intelligent and beautiful angel?'

'Never did seem very fair to me either.' I nodded. 'Still, since it is God after all, I felt I had to give him a fair chance, because according to all the church teachings he sent his only son to die for us.'

'Well, I have a simple answer to that,' Margaret replied.

'Really?' My eyebrows raised.

'Yes.' Margaret set down her cup, looked up at me steadily and stated flatly, 'Not my mythology.'

'Like in College? When all religion is presented as mythology?'

'That is one way to look at it, but for me it is very simple.' A light seemed to fill Margaret's eyes as she continued. 'For me, the earth and the stars are alive. For me, this world, this reality, is full of mystery and wisdom to be discovered. For me, a Goddess brought forth all life and gives to all people the gifts of her nature.'

'Wow…' I expressed honestly.

We were silent a moment.

'I was raised Lutheran,' Margaret announced.

'So was I.'

'So, here we are.'

We both laughed.

Then a thoughtful look crossed Margaret's face and she continued speaking. 'When I was a small child, I assumed that everyone saw the world as I did. I did not understand the strange looks I sometimes got, or why my mother would say with a wave of her hand, "*Oh, she is just such a creative and imaginative child.*" I was told this was a good thing, but every time I heard it I got a knot in my stomach, because it didn't feel right to me.

'When I was about five, I told a child in Sunday school to be nice to a girl called Lisa because "she is dealing with a lot and has a headache". Lisa had only just walked in with her mother, so I was asked how I knew this by the child next to me. I answered back in surprise, "Just look at her colors. I know some people do not pay attention, but it is easy to see today." The child asked what I was talking about.

'"The rainbow colors around everyone," I answered. "If you are sad or ill, they can be grey or muddy-looking. Don't you see them at least sometimes?"

'Some other children approached us, and they too were

asked by my friend and I: "Do you see rainbow colors around people sometimes?"

'The question soon flew about the room until finally, even the teacher knew. She came to me concerned and wrote a note to my mother to get my eyes checked.'

'So, you see auras?' I asked. 'That's what it's called, right?'

'Yes, as long as I can remember,' Margaret replied. 'Other gifts came later as I grew older.'

'Is that how you knew you were a witch?'

'It's a part of it, but you can be a gifted Christian with the gift of prophecy, just like St Paul says in the Bible, and it does not necessarily mean you are a witch as long as you are speaking for God. Though some will always see you as an evil witch, good or bad, it *does* matter what you say or call yourself.' She sighed. 'Do you feel you are a witch?'

'I guess that depends,' I responded. 'In first grade, kids called my mother and I the Nazi witches. Sometimes they called me a gypsy witch as well. It was partly because of my way with animals. Bringing my pet bat to school in first grade to educate my classmates did not have the effect I hoped for.'

Margaret's face broke into a huge grin. 'I imagine not.'

'So, what do you think?' I asked.

'I think that this is an exciting time of exploration for you,' she offered. 'I think you should educate yourself with an open mind and see what lights you up inside and gives you joy, fulfillment, and peace.'

I raised my eyebrows. 'Is becoming a witch following a religion?'

'For some yes, it is, but for others it's more a way of life, like the way Native Americans live,' Margaret responded. 'It's also the path of many poets and artists.'

'I was told as a young child that being an artist brings you closer to God.'

'That is true, but it's still a matter of culture, perspective and experience.'

I looked around the room. It was filled to the brim with books, art and crafts. Varuka had found a perch to survey us from and looked at me as if she too expected an answer.

'I guess you could recommend some books to read.'

'Indeed, I can.'

Margaret reached over and placed three books in front of me. *The Spiral Dance*, *Greek History and Mythology* and a heavy tome called *The White Goddess* by Robert Graves. 'You're not homeless, I take it.'

'No, I am not.'

'Then I'll let you borrow these and come back with at least two of them in a week. Otherwise, I will turn you into a toad or something else unpleasant.'

Her eyes glittered with humor and determination, leaving me no doubt that toad-dom would surely be mine should I fail to comply.

'You sing? Draw? Write?' she asked.

'A little of all of it,' I replied.

'Of course.' She grinned. 'Then bring me a song or something you wrote as well, and we'll then do a reading next time.'

'A reading? Like a séance?

'No, something far more useful. Write down your birthday for me, please.'

I was surprised, and a touch confused. 'So, you think I should become a witch?'

'That depends on you. All I can say is, by the look of you, there is a lot in you that is crying to come out, and you are trying, like all of humanity, to be free. You're just a little more aware than some people. I don't waste my time with stupid or insincere people, especially when they're not paying me.' She chuckled as she headed me toward the door weighed down with the books.

'What's the most important thing I need to learn to become a witch?' I blurted out at the door.

Margaret stopped in her tracks and said without hesitation. 'Becoming a wordsmith.'

'Like a poet?' I was a bit surprised at this answer.

Margaret drew herself up a little taller, it seemed, and in a tone of absolute authority conveyed firmly, 'Therein is the well where people seek wisdom and also to learn how to express love. See you next week.' And she closed the door.

I stood there slightly open-mouthed, before wandering home, deep in thought, realizing that there was much for me to learn.

The Girl Becomes a Young Woman

Margaret about to perform a handfasting

It was from this time that my world bloomed into a whole new life, with a succession of adventures that I chronicled in a series of articles for Punk Globe Magazine, called *San Francisco 1978.* Margaret also eventually introduced me to the lawyer she was legal secretary for. Attorney John Doyle was a unique man from a notable Irish family from Long Island. He had been born at the naval base in the Philippines right before WWII and, despite being very hearing impaired from birth, he'd become a spectator of history from a young age, witnessing the bombing of Pearl Harbor and many other historic events and people. At the time when we met, he needed help to take care of his father, the late Vice Admiral James Henry Doyle, who was one of our military greats from WWII's naval Battle of

Guadalcanal, on up to the nuclear bombing of Hiroshima and Nagasaki in Japan. During the Korean War he'd been in charge of the Inchon Landing and the Hungnam evacuation. It was an honor and privilege to help take care of him in the last year of his life.

The Admiral told me stories of his friendship with General MacArthur, the aftermath of the bombing of Japan and what it was like being at the Japanese surrender. He spoke also of the terrible burden of sending young men into battle.

John and I at our west-coast Handfasting conducted by Margaret

A few weeks after his father's funeral, in Annapolis at the Naval academy, I was surprised and pleased when John showed up at my door. We started dating and, despite our age difference, found we had much in common. We married a year and a day later; first in the spring, with a jump over the broom handfasting in San Francisco and then, in the Fall, at home in Albion, in the Methodist College church. Both ceremonies felt so right and were a lot of fun for our family and friends.

Back in San Francisco, John settled into doing criminal appeals. Always one to help the underdog, whether in jails or helping a cause. A few years later, he and I, along with Kathy Peck, created H.E.A.R (Hearing Education Awareness for Rockers). One would think that with becoming a lawyer's wife, my life would settle into a predictable pattern, but such is not the fate of singers, poets or witches.

By the time I married John, I had learned much from Margaret and was also working for a metaphysical and ecumenical church. It was also around this time that I first met the poet Victor Anderson and his wife Cora. They practiced a magical tradition called Feri or Faery. After spending twenty years as both a friend and a student of theirs, I was entrusted with Victor's last words and teachings, which was published in 2017 as *Victor Anderson an American Shaman*.

During this period, I also sang in several bands or on my own. I worked as a metaphysical minster and assisted my husband at his law office. We also continued to help Kathy Peck, from the all-girl Punk band *The Contractions*, with the non-profit H.E.A.R. It was such a full and exciting time, during which I did so many things, singing in bands such as 'Lil' Susie and the Sparkletones' with Susie Davis and later with Kathy Peck in 'Tammy Why Not and the Bushwackers', with Senorita Carmelita (who was yours truly). Kathy and I created TV spots about hearing loss for VH1 and MTV. We even collaborated with a film crew from Sweden to create the documentary *Can't Hear You Knocking, a film about hearing lossand issues among musicians.* By the 90s, John and I also started raising a child, our beloved Kaitlin, and I was an Aunty or Godmother to several more children. Looking back, it is hard to believe that I burned the candle at both ends for so long. Yet, little did I realize that it was my way of embracing the never-ending holy grail of life. I drank deep of its cup… and still do.

Our Autumn wedding in Michigan

The Wisdom of the Poet

Not long after marrying John, I found myself in Victor Anderson's 'throne room'. That is, his living room, with the poet and sage perched on his beloved rocking chair. I was handed a sheet of paper with one poem on it.

'I would like you to read this and then tell me what it says,' requested Victor.

I quickly glanced over the poem. It was a simple and direct poem about love and loss. Victor's face was expressionless as he waited for me to finish and speak. I wondered, briefly, if there was going to be some sort of trick. Perhaps the poem contained some nearly imponderable allegory, or hidden symbolism, and this was a test to see if I had the smarts and necessary sensitivity to glean the more profound aspects of it.

'I think I'd better read it again before I answer you,' I offered Victor prudently.

He rocked ever so slightly and patiently as I studied the poem. I looked for hidden symbols and occult meaning and, though one could color it that way, somehow the most striking thing about the poem were the deep human feelings artfully poured out upon the page.

I knew that to try and sound worldly would be a mistake. *If I'm missing something, oh well, I'm young. To be honest will be better than grasping for some sort of profundity, which would make me look quite silly.*

'It's about love,' I ventured, 'and does not say much about the other person's feelings. The writer feels great loss, but the poem also implies he does not regret the relationship.'

Victor smiled and rocked a little more in his chair. 'Very good. You are not as messed up as many people,' he remarked, with the slightest bitterness in his tone.

I could not help but laugh. 'There might be some who'd argue that with you. I've been a bit of a strange child as long as I can remember, which is a pretty long time.'

I jumped as he pounded his cane on the floor.

'Do not,' Victor thundered, 'debase and confuse yourself with either false modesty or the prattling of others with false intentions!'

I was slightly shaken by this outburst. 'I don't understand. What do you mean?'

Victor took a deep breath and said evenly, 'In this world there are all kinds of people from the sciences to the arts to what people now call spirituality digging and rooting about for what they think is deeper meaning or hidden secrets, instead of seeing what is really there right under their noses.'

'I see,' I said cautiously.

'Yes, you do, but you have a secondary infection.' Victor replied.

'A what?' My eyebrows raised.

Victor took another deep breath. 'What I mean is that, as with this poem, you can see things for what they really are, and I am willing to bet this goes on many levels as it does with me? Yet, like so many young people of today you also have allowed yourself to become polluted by the dubious opinions of others that make you second-guess or doubt yourself.'

'Why are these opinions dubious? They can come from very smart people or people that love you - even one's family.'

A wide grin broke out on Victor's face. He rocked evenly in his chair before pointing out, 'That's what makes it so insidious and dangerous.'

He went on to explain that with few exceptions most people need to affirm their little piece of life and reality by making sure that those around them are either the same or similar in outlook, opinion and talent.

'Therefore, people who have the sensitivity to see wider, deeper and further, or who have talents and gifts that set them a little apart, are often seen as threats. This can become especially obvious if those talents are publicly observable. Consequently, those who are more perceptive, talented or gifted must be brought in line as quickly as possible. The best way to do this is to humiliate them, make them doubt themselves until they start to do the work for you by putting themselves down in order to be accepted by those around them. In the long run, if not freed by their better nature, these gifted people often destroy themselves through this inflicted confusion and bitterness, which in turn leads to becoming embroiled with drugs and drink. Ultimately, the vultures come in to pick over their kill.'

'Why would someone who loves you do such a thing to you?' I asked.

'Mostly because those people foolishly talk themselves into believing they are doing this for your own good!' replied Victor emphatically. 'They think they're manifesting the gift of a swift kick or a slap for your betterment, when their real and underlying motivation is, at best, fear for themselves. At worst, it's plain old jealousy or malicious control. This is a type of evil that people do all the time, so we are used to it and do not see it for what it is.'

I sighed. 'That's pretty harsh, Victor.'

'People make life harsh for themselves, let alone each other, much more than it ever need be. But then again, it does make for some mighty damn fine poetry.' He burst into a joyous laugh and all traces of bitterness flew away from his face like startled sparrows.

The Trees

One of the giant Firs where we once lived

On November 7, 2009, I was living in Oregon when I became the bystander to an awesome event: nature showed its astonishing power and scope. Now, on the surface one could say: *Oh, come on, nature is nature and it is what it is even when it is, shall we say... impressive?* Well yes, impressive is one word for it, but I am now exploring this event with a larger lens as I write about it.

Out there in Oregon the land was still lush. Thick with trees and ferns. There was a growing movement to lumber responsibly, to farm and ranch organically when possible. In other words, to live as best as one can in harmony with wildlife and nature in general. Sadly, this wisdom was not extended to the Native Americans, who had been living in the region for most likely longer than eight thousand years. In the 1800s, the local tribe was removed from their land alongside a river in Yamhill County. They were given the name Yamhill and taken to a reservation where their population has dwindled to under a hundred, today. The trees, not succumbing to the needs and whims of man or to time and tide, became the mute sentinels to witness the changing landscape and humankind's shifting habits and trends.

The lore of native tribal cultures around the world, not just here in America, tells us that trees have a spirit or consciousness. They feel and react slowly because their awareness is encased in their wooden structure. Yet, shamans warn that these spirits are old and powerful and not to be taken for granted. Trees, like animals, sustain us day to day with their food and medicinal qualities, but their influence and gifts to us are more steady, reliable, longer lasting, and subtle. They provide us with protective shade and offer housing for other living wildlife. Their roots hold the soil, preventing erosion.

In our region, fir and evergreen trees of several types are common, such trees usually living eighty to one hundred and forty years on average. Yet some become grandfather trees that can live and grow closer to two hundred years or more. Here is a story of two such trees.

A small group of trees stood amazingly tall by a little cabin. Over time, as owners of the land changed, so did the weather, and the number of the trees had dwindled down to just two giant firs. These trees were loved, admired and even a touch feared, since their looming presence was an ever-present danger to the cabin that was now my friend's naturopathic clinic. The surrounding area was a bustle of horses, children, dogs and cats, with the comings and goings of clients and residents.

I was staying in a small trailer down the road from this cabin, tucked away in the forest, at a distance around the length of three football fields. A few days before, I had taken some pictures. It had been one of those outstandingly beautiful days. I had been almost giddy with my freedom to walk about the property taking pictures instead of the usual nose to the grindstone routine. I snapped away, wandering down to the clinic and back, taking pictures of the great trees and the surrounding countryside. I was very happy with the images of nature's perfection I had captured on my trusty phone and I felt renewed. So, imagine my shock when I came home a day later to find one of the great trees on the ground with lumbermen sawing it into planks. My friend, the owner of the surrounding property, was picking up smaller branches.

'Oh my, what happened?' I asked. 'Was the tree sick?'

She nodded and one of the tree men explained;

'Old age and bugs.'

'And it was leaning, too,' my friend added.

I understood that my friend, being a doctor and a longtime owner of horses, had to make difficult decisions from time to time, and this was a practical necessity of life in the country. She was turning the tree to lumber so it would be put to good use at its home, which was also practical and an acknowledgement to honor its spirit. My eyes turned to the one remaining tree. It had an elderberry growing next to it and I fleetingly wondered if the tree was aware of the elderberry, let alone that its twin fir was now gone.

I drove home with an odd feeling prickling deep in my mind, but I could not define it, so I let it go. Once in my trailer, I brought up my pictures of the last few days and was surprised to see that, back in the shadows of one picture, I could see the cut tree had indeed been in trouble. At the time I had taken the picture I was so delighted that the elderberries were still in fruit I'd not paid attention to the firs. All in all, I think of myself as an aware and observant person, so I was a bit shocked I had not noticed the failing health of the giant fir.

The next few days passed quickly. The front of the clinic was cleaned in the nick of time, as the first fall rains were expected that weekend. When Saturday came, the rain kept me indoors. This was accompanied by thunder, which was neither very frequent nor very loud, but my instincts were telling me to be cautious because my animals were acting nervously. As a precaution, I had shut down my computer and turned off the television. I felt melancholy and restless, which prompted me to call my parents. I was then talking to my father on the phone. Of course, the usual 'How is the weather' question had to be addressed and gotten through. Yet, when I told my parents about the rain, they were concerned with me being on the phone. My mother reminded me of her own mother's encounters with ball lightning in Germany. My father asked if I had a lightning rod on the house, and just as I was assuring him that such was the case, several things all happened at the same time.

I felt I was somehow in the middle of a movie like The Matrix, because – for a few seconds – reality changed.

First, I heard the loudest sound I've ever heard in my life. The ground and house shook with the force of what felt like a 5.5 earthquake. Outdoors, everything turned a bright electric blue. This eerie blue light danced and flashed throughout my house, while I watched the glass explode from a large picture frame, just before the whole piece, picture and frame, flew off the wall and crashed to the floor. At the same time, the lights and phone went out.

At this point, my cats dashed across the broken glass. I realized I had no shoes on and that it was possible a large fir that stood by my house had been hit by the lightning. Inspired by the fear of a huge tree falling on my head, I somehow managed to leap across the broken glass, hightailing it after my cats. We ran to the other side of the house and all leapt onto my bed, hoping it would provide comfort and safety. Only seconds of cowering on the bed had passed before the sky opened like a faucet, pouring rain so hard I could not even see the woods through my window.

'OH NO! The doggies and the chickens!' I cried out, jumping off the bed. With shaking hands, I pulled on some shoes. I looked at the cats. They stared at me with frozen dilated owl eyes that said, 'We are not moving.'

I peeked out of my front window expecting to see the chickens either dead or fainted, but to my relief and amusement the chickens and the dogs were huddled together near the front door. I opened the door to reassure the chickens, who clearly also wanted to be allowed in the house. Leaving the disappointed birds outside, I herded the whimpering doggies to a glass-free spot before quickly sweeping up the broken shards.

Then I took stock of the house. My snake had been shaken from his slumber but otherwise seemed his usual serene self. To my surprise, the phone I had on speaker started beeping and the lights flickered back on. My heart was still beating hard as I realized how much had happened in just the last couple of minutes.

I grabbed the phone as I went to another window to check the closest trees, but it was raining too hard to see anything. I wondered if my house had taken the hit directly. I dialed my nearest neighbor, but the phone just rang, so I assumed she was at work and that her child was with friends, it being the weekend. The rain was still pouring yet I was able to call my parents back to let them know I was all right. It was then I noticed that my head hurt, and my ears were ringing.

'Remember how you always told me you hoped I'd never know what it feels like when a bomb goes off?' I said to my mother, who had been a child in Germany during the Second World War. 'Well, I think I got a taste of it.'

By the time I hung up on that phone call the deluge had let up a bit, so I put on a raincoat and stepped outside. I trotted around and about the house and my neighbor's barn. Nothing looked amiss, nothing was sizzling or burning. I was on my porch, shaking the rain off, when I heard the phone ring. It was my doctor friend's husband.

'Are you all right?' he asked.

I told him I thought my house had been hit by lightning. He laughed a little as I told him, in a big rush, about the house shaking and the exploding glass. Then he told me that the lightning had struck the tree in front of his wife's clinic. It had exploded with heavy force, taking a small transformer with it. The clinic had six people inside it at the time, including my friend the doctor. The force of the blast knocked her into a wall, but no one was injured; they were all just very shaken up. The neighbor's young children had thought it was God ending the world, while others had thought the cause was a bomb or a fallen plane. My friend's husband told me to wait at least fifteen minutes before I went to look around, because men were moving the downed power-lines. I waited and then walked the length of three football fields down to the office.

The top half of the remaining tree was in bits all over the ground. My friend's truck was beat up by a large falling branch. About seventy feet or more of this huge tree trunk was lying some distance away from the clinic, even leaving room for other cars to get around once the debris had been moved, which people were already working on. The blast had happened when everyone, including two children, had just gone inside the clinic. Also, it had happened right before the mail person would have brought their deliveries to the mailboxes near where the great tree had once stood.

My eyes widened as I beheld all the squished mailboxes; they were just twisted or flattened metal. My head still hurt, and my ears were still ringing slightly, yet the miracle of the moment was not lost on me or anyone else.

Someone behind me asked, 'Don't you think it's kind of bizarre, and maybe more than a coincidence, that after all these years this tree gets hit by lightning right after its twin is cut down?'

'I know,' I answered. 'It's like the tree called down the lightning because it didn't want to be here anymore.'

'I'm not usually such a romantic, but it does seem that way,' was one person's reply.

'The real amazing thing is that nothing hit the clinic and no people or animals were hurt,' I added.

We all nodded, still in shock at this demonstration of nature's raw power and rare mercy. All of us got busy picking up the smaller branches, after which I returned to my house and my critters.

In the next few days the huge tree trunk was cut into planks. The mailboxes were dealt with, as well as a few cars with broken windows, the downed power line and the transformer. The land soon returned to its own rhythm and pace.

I wrote down this story and pondered about the larger picture of the event. Was the lightning strike an 'Act of God' as the children thought? The insurance companies covering the situation would undoubtedly characterize this incident as such too. Was this fierce blast a message or a reminder of how fragile we are in the face of the forces of nature, forces we can only slightly and temporarily control, such as through seeding clouds or building levees? Was it perhaps a cruel and capricious reminder of a random universe that rubs our noses in the 'too bad, too sad' fact that life can end in the blink of an eye? Or instead, could it be possible that what had been thought of as a merely romantic notion **is** much closer to the truth than we think? When one takes the time to think about it, does not an ant seek to live when it falls in water? Does not the smallest cell fight for survival in its host? Do not the planets and stars themselves form, find their pattern and pace in the long ages, only to find change and thereafter their own ultimate demise?

Is it so far-fetched to think that a tree was seeking its release and freedom, that some essence of its heart or soul called upon its God in nature to free it, for it now sought union with its own kindred? Could it be that this call was not one of sorrow, but a statement of its completion and that the time had come to move on?

In the passing of the years how can we know the effects of what was planted by the roots of those immense firs, such as the lovely little labyrinth with a garden of healing herbs and a feeding station for birds? How can we know the effect of the long years of murmured voices that spoke prayers, hummed songs and in their own human way did the best they could for the garden and the trees? Could it be that somehow the trees knew or sensed this? Is not this flow of observation the awareness where the wellspring of all poetry, spiritual awareness, healing and hope awakens?

Maybe only the trees truly know . . .

The Poems of
Cornelia Benavidez

Poems Of and About Long Ago

I wrote my first poem at the age of eleven. At twelve, I began writing stories, including a whole movie script. I wrote with great fervor, which really worried my parents because I did almost nothing but write for that whole summer.

Poetry took a back seat until I started playing guitar a few years later. This prompted me, when I was around seventeen, to begin writing lyric poetry to accompany my music.

In college, from eighteen on, writing music and poetry became a large part of my life. Thereafter, even today, as I go through boxes or peek at a beloved old book, I still find envelopes, napkins, and bits of paper with poems and songs scribbled here and there from long ago. Leaving Albion had been hard in many ways yet, in San Francisco, there was the taste and flavor of Europe with so much creative possibility. I so wanted to become a part of its story.

Exile

I close my eyes,
Try to imagine
Your distant shore.

I pray that it is a sweet retreat,
A warm womb to nurture
Your bruised soul.

I shy away from loss,
Dwell not on the human folly
That takes the best of us
Into Exile.

Memories

Sometimes even now when I close my eyes
I drift back to Albion, my childhood town.
There's pain but mostly joy and wonder.

I watch a wild-haired child exploring woods and cornfields,
Bunnies scatter and blue jays scold over her head.
Mulberries, blackberries fill hungry and thirsty lips.

In the distance stands one of God's many houses,
Where I once sat in long hard pews, curls tamed,
daydreaming of Christmas Eve,
full of candlelight magic and soaring hymns.

Music filled the air in Albion,
from the wind in its trees and rivers,
Marching bands, symphonies,
Mother at the piano, radios blaring,
Boys and girls strumming guitars
and Papa singing in the garden.

Childhood was full of fireflies,
frogs and pesky mosquitoes.
Swimming, holding my sister's hand.
Old men told fishing tales.
I am taught the Pony and the Monkey
in a friend's basement.

We camped in backyards
as brothers play midnight monsters.
Mayday and square dancing
turned into the Boogaloo and the Sissy Strut.
School went from Duck Duck Goose
to duck and cover under desks.

Cornelia Benavidez

Horse and bike-riding,
the first tastes of freedom were blowing in my hair.
Teachers and politics, bomb scares but,
still giggling, we filed outside.
State projects, carnivals, the circus.
Then someone spun the bottle.

And suddenly we were not the same,
as swimsuits turned to bikinis.
Boys took refuge in sports, music or science.
Girls sighed.
At weddings, we watched grandparents
dance in the Armory.

We jumped on fifteen
and we lived the High School Musical,
The field and stage our new home.
Albion rocked,
Controversies to its triumphant wins
all heralded by song and dance.

Scattered so many kinds of birds
near and far once caps were tossed.
Seasons changed in so many ways yet,
in this stately college town,
Albion rivers still run, children play
as parents still garden to the music.

The Methodist Steeple on Albion College Campus

Cornelia Benavidez

Christmas in Germany

The tree was in the waiting room
Behind the tall French doors,
Full of sparkling mementos
Of the sweet things of life.

Its light flickers of another place
And of another time.
The room smells deep of pine
Its colors a feast for the eyes.

I see myself coming home
From church, in cold and snow,
Filled with music, candle light glow
Grandfather at the door.

The most beautiful tree
I will evermore see
Will be that one in Germany
Living on in the child in me.

Fire

Only a babe in arms
I reached for the bright blue flames
Hissing under the black tea kettle
Mother says FIRE hot danger death
I always looked back with longing eyes
Whispering Hot Hot under my breath

On plump sturdy little legs
Months later, on the oven I lean
Reaching up toward the blazing blue
Chanting hot hot as I test my tip toes
Mother lifted me up saying yes hot hot
Sadly, the meaning you know not
She took my little hand
Ever so quick I touched the glowing pot
My eyes grow huge and tear-filled
Then cool water and kisses the pain killed
I point to the flames and the singing pot
Pretty......... Blue...........danger.......Hot!
There was born respect for fire's
beauty and temptation
The thin path between wisdom and fascination

Years pass, a little boy in a yard lights a match
Holds the blazing yellow orange and neon blue
Close to his eyes I fear his eyebrows will catch
Then drops from stung fingers onto the grass
He stamps quick on the white Smokey wisps
This is not a good idea I say calmly
You are a goody two shoes he says firmly
Fire is dangerous to the playful say I
So is water snapped back the bold boy child

You can save yourself in water
You cannot swim in flames I pout
Smarty pants always the last word he shouts
His words sting as the dinner bell sounds
Quick he grabbed my hand good
Dragged me to supper and wolfed down his food
Then his uncle burst in with a bucket of sand
Whose child's hide tonight must I tan!
For the curiosity kills the cat with desire
All eyes turned to me, but my mother says
Not her, for she knows the truth of fire

With growing speed the years start to turn
Warm sun on summer golden skin
Fireworks sparkle without and within
A bonfire night again fire make me yearn
A crackling campfire with a moonlit kiss
Heart's a runaway flame and a cool bliss
Fire is comfort, Fire is pain
Fire is loss, yet it can be gain
The fire within gives the courage to fight
The fire of passion to make things right
Temptations are mostly the little burn
That tempers us and makes us learn
As I was once told it's a wild-wild world
Mother and father pray I pay not too high a price
As I struggle with watching the dark and light
Desire and risk and the quest for wisdom
To know your soul and find fulfillment
From Pandora's Box to the tempting stranger
Reaching for my hand...
Hot....Pretty...Danger!

Today's Memorial

Today I remember:
All the red paper poppies pinned on lapels,
All the toes tipping over street curbs
as the parade goes by.
I remember people in the crowd with misty eyes,
Speaking in hushed tones of lost sons,
fathers, lovers and brothers.
My father and the many of his family served with honor,
My husband's father and brother
each gave a lifetime of service.
I think of those who came home whole
to parents, family and friends,
While many came home wounded
in body, heart and mind.
We honor them all, especially all those we will never find.
May we remember why the flowers and flags
spring from their grave,
All the young vital lives that could not be saved,
And know all those buried from shore to shore
Are each a prayer that war shall be no more.

Old Glory on a stormy day

Rubik's Cube

I wonder where the truth lies
That it seems so hard to find
Like hidden in a maze or puzzle
While you lose your mind.

They tell you to relax
In this world of confusion
While you're only fighting
For your spot of illusion.

Don't tell me I'm crazy
For questioning truths
Tearing into its words
And seeking its roots.

Knowledge ends fear
So many have said it
Yet I have also heard
Ignorance is blessed.

Cornelia Benavidez

It's All a Part of Me

Born in the land of dreams after the Great War
Of a mother whose beauty hid the scars she bore.
Papa held the pride of the people of the land,
Hid his sorrows by working hard with his hands.
And it is all a part of me

Mama's blood flowed strong
from the Rhine to Baltic States.
Papa's ran from Indian lands back to Spain and old Egypt.
I look in the mirror to find every trace.
My sister shares its heart but not the same face.

I smile at the wonder of such history in our veins,
How we are so different and yet so much the same.
Somewhere inside me there is a part of all my kin
And somewhere in you a piece of me under your skin.

Mama could dance like a leaf blowing in a breeze.
When Papa sang even the birds listened from the trees.
Every sweet moment like crystal in my mind
And every sorrow a teardrop frozen in time.

Born in the hope of peace after the Great War,
Mother sewed her strength in the clothes that we wore.
Father long searched for our place in the sun.
Yes, it was found but how hard it was won.
And it's all a part of me, it's all a part of me.

Mutti dancing in a field after WWII

Dancing

The moments I could dance
Were moments of quintessence
Where I felt whole and complete
In those precious minutes
I was a flash of perfection
Somehow in time with cosmic order
Aligned with soul, mind and body
The brief smile of your approval

The moments I could dance
I felt power like lightening in the air
My arms turned to wings
Feet no more feeling floor
My heart sang the beat
I am wind, I am song
Flying I have become love
For the moment to be the universe

The Eye in the Needle

You laughed
As you told me about it
You laughed even though
Not a trace of you had been spared
From the dark steel finger
Its delights and dark poison
A hard-cruel lover that you embrace
With every available opening
In your sweet body, it demanded more

You laughed
As you told me about it
How you offered your life's blood
A willing sacrifice
You laugh to hide the agony
And the bitter cold, cold fear
In the palm of your aching hand
A Demon of Pain
In a body of Love

The Weight of an End

You told me once again how close you came,
As if I have not heard the rats that scratch upon your door.
I listen with serene painful patience to hear it all once more.
Yes, women will bear all fear and pain just to hold a child.
Perhaps this is another way to give forth and sustain life.

Drunk on Pineapple Orange and Vitamin C

So, are things unfolding as they should?
Are the pieces firm in their little squares
Awaiting the next hand to guide them?
Do I wait to feel the creeping vine of bitterness?
Am I a noble experiment that has faltered,
Now a loose pawn watching on the sidelines?
Are we sensation with no deeper purpose?
Is there actually no true good or evil?
Such considerations bring insanity and damnation.
Did the act of creation give birth to its own arrogance?
Did it taint eternity with its own folly?
Let us all become Saviors, then.
Is all pain our fear of lack of power,
And our anger lack of grace and courage?
Dare we to save creation and ourselves?
Do we live within a trap and paradox?
Do I dare say we can comprehend?
Ah... Satan, sin is but the fragment of daring
That you had to pay the price for.

Moment

Coit Tower stands porcelain against the silvered sky
The Gulls rise raucous from their portside perch
Another fog-kissed sunset
Babies wrapped by mothers
Lovers wrapped in each other
Somewhere the heart of San Francisco lies beating
Its rhythm deep, quiet and steady
Keeping time beneath the bay's moaning warning horns

Cornelia Benavidez

Turning Point

There comes a time when you just turn and walk away,
Not believing anymore in all you once knew.
Words just words are what you have heard.
You find yourself standing alone
And fingers point only at you.
Yes, maybe I am for a lot of things,
But I also know what I am not,
For I have compared myself to what I see around me.
To know my mind and what I got
I would rather dance on the edge of sanity
To embrace the God of my heart.
Does it not all come down to the changes
The quest for being free and winning wisdom?
Knowledge once meant to know the mind of the divine:
How much lost and forgotten has mankind.

Sidewinder

Sidewinder you thought you had me fooled
Sidewinder playing it so cool
You're a gentle, twisting, choking vine
Saw you coming from behind

You say; you can do it like an art
You can do it all for your pleasure
I say I'll end up paying the price
Measure for measure.

Sidewinder
I know the score
I laughed at your face
And showed you the door

Considerations

Poetry teaches us in every step of its creation. By expressing itself in an outer tangible form it gives us courage to face ourselves, confronting inner demons as well as deep emotional secrets of both pain and wisdom. It teaches us to self-examine and to think, not only outside of society's boxes, but also the boxes we impose upon ourselves. Through poetry we mull over our emotional reactions, either to hold close our words like a treasure with a code only we might know or, perhaps, it inspires us to reach out and experience life all the more. We test and push at boundaries and dogmas. Yet still we endeavor to access a balance, between what seems logical against what may be possible, be it in anything from love to spirituality, science and imagination to tangible practical invention. We seek out what is beautiful and wondrous for it expands something inside us that we instinctively feel is sacred.

Sometimes, the only way to convey to your own self, let alone others, of how an experience made you feel is to write it down. Some of these experiences can only be cast in poetry. It might manifest in other ways down the road – a song, a painting, instrumental music – yet poetry is often the first capture of the snapshots that define who we are and what we are striving to become.

Statement

It is said that nothing is truly known
Except for all the rules and games
And the patterns that they show.
And it is said that we are always alone;
If you wish something different
It might be at the price of your soul.

So, do I live, do I feel, and do I decide
Who I am, how I will, how I live or die?
Can I heal, can I create, can I not conceive
Who you are, and what is really real?

It is said that life is heaven sent,
Except for those who say
That it is hell that we are in.
And it is said that you must do as you are told
Yet we so wish to be free
From the moment we are born.

Well, I reach
And I touch
I believe in my heart
That I love
And I care
And that is my start
Yes, I live
I am
I must decide
How I will
How I choose
How I will live this life.

Cornelia Benavidez

Looking Back

I will not be fearful of my memories,
That freezing of a point in time
To collect and capture and be mine.

A rose, a vista, the smile of a child,
San Francisco captured in the mists,
Life's fleeting banquet of gifts.

I will not be fearful of the memories
In captured thoughts in my mind,
Nor of photographs or written lines.

I cannot be fearful of my human purpose,
Nor the catalog of one's own creativity
To point my course through all eternity.

For Stephen Stills

Hey baby it's been a long time gone
Yet here you are still rockin' on.
Don't you feel how we still need you
After our eyes got glazed and dazed
And for a while you hardened your heart.

We all must pick ourselves up now
From life's bruises and soul bleeds.
We are still alive and it's a new day.
Each of us have a voice to join to yours,
Keep showing the way, keep showing the way.

This Way and That

The bird flew by so quickly
Like a fleeting glance
And love came just as swiftly
As a melody by chance
And flowers bloom and fade
While the wind blows in the change
From this way and that
From this way and that

The song was o'er so quickly
Like a gentle smile
While my heart debated fiercely
If I was worth your time
And seasons will come and go
It is rumored we all grow old
From this way and that
From this way and that

The sun dropped down so quickly
As it kissed the sea
Perhaps ten thousand sunsets
Were witnessed just by me
And the moon caresses
A glittered sky
While I am wondering why
This way and that
This way and that

Sunset off Ocean Beach in San Francisco

The Voice

The voice of avoidance haunted me
Like a bad smell from an unidentified source,
Like an ache with a barometer's rise and fall.
I became the bloodhound, a courage forced
By air unbreathable, by stagnant doubt.

The voice recites memory's art,
Painted by telescoped eyes and emotion's brush,
Fixed statuettes in the mind's museum,
Dance to life by the wand of feeling and
Transfer to me their frigid being.

The voice condemns yet longs, determined
Seeds crippled by words then scrubbed with reason
That never quite flowered in their season.
I see in the yawning past subtle silent tragedies
Of familial curse and hope's endless pleas.

My voice silenced - not even an aching song
Frightened out the hero in avoidance halls.
Experience kissed by visions divine
Sets free the tangled echoes in this life,
It germinates the heart of soul and mind
Illumines the path to what at last is mine.

Cornelia Benavidez

Three Wishes for John

If I had three wishes
And a bright green genie
Floating in blue smoke
I'd wish for your health and healing
All in body, mind, and heart.

If I had three wishes
And a bright green genie
Thundering smoke and fire
I'd ask to be very, very brave
And really know my heart's desire.

If I had three wishes
And a bright green genie
With wisdom galore
I'd wish for all the time we need
To free the genie's soul.

So, if I first free the genie's soul
Would he remain true and whole?
And grant the wishes one and two?
Ah, such fairness, so sublime
Make angels laugh divine.

For Leggs

A wonderful horse
Blessed were we by your great heart.
Patiently you let us roam
Through field, forest and sunlit pastures.
Blessed were we by your strong back,
Gentle eyes that let us speak secrets
Sharing wordlessly both joy and pain.

May your spirit arise to the wind,
Be embraced by thy patron Goddess Epona
To run free in the lands of summer
To receive the promise of nature's renewal.
Hail and farewell good friend.
Let us have hope in the mystery and
In the ways of divine time and tide to meet again.

Sweet and kind Leggs

Cornelia Benavidez

Yesterday

Yesterday the sun shone
Through the trees
Like cupid's arrows.

Two mated robins
Sang of devotion
As tree frogs chorused.

I thought of your lifetime
Deserts, waterfalls of mystery
Now spirit in the thunder.

I Am a Mother

I say this as simple fact
I am a Mother.
Though my womb is unstretched
I am a Mother.
By every child and living thing
I have hugged, healed, disciplined and kissed
I am a Mother as I pray for all I so miss.
I am Mother to whose hand I hold
Be they child, man, woman or the very old.
I am a Mother
For all those who I have cradled in my arms.
I am a Mother to whom I have raised
And protected from harm.
I am a Mother
By every tender touch and by every tear
I have taught, laughed, cooked and cleaned
I am a Mother.
When I walk the forests, I kiss the earth
For she is my Mother and I am hers.

Mother's Day

My mother loved sunsets: it was a time to be grateful
for the day you had lived.
My mother loved trees, saying each one is a gift.
My mother loved mountains, a living symbol
of what is strong and pure.
My mother loved the wind,
a hint of the power of our souls.
My mother loved birds for they fly so fearless
to sing songs till they die.
My mother loved to dance,
therein was her peace and happiness.
My mother loved so many things:
her family, her friends, the Lord in her heart.
My mother loved life for it is all a divine art.
Happy Mother's Day, Mutti, wherever you are.

Teleport Time

Yesterday an early evening sun
Glittered through the trees.
My sister over a thousand miles away
Held up an iPad to a storm-ripped sky.
We smiled in satisfaction at the beauty
And power in place and time.
We cannot teleport ourselves yet,
We can send our reality wherever we please.

Cornelia Benavidez

Cigs

Cigarettes give us odd powers
And perhaps the illusion of deep thought
A smoky veil conjures don't see me

Not Today
Not Today

Cigarettes are the observer's comfort
And arid subtle reminders of human stress
All the feelings of rage and bliss to keep in check

Stay detached
Stay detached

The smell of cigarettes gives rise to old debates
It dances its social curse through romantic lore
and human waste
Its perfume, like us, lingers
and always is wanting more and we...

Walk away or stay
Walk away or stay

You Can See It in Her Eyes

Kaitlin

The babe had been napping.
When she was first placed in my arms
The long dark lashes fluttered
I was captured in pools of my reflection,
Diving into the soul in her eyes.
Our spirits bonded and we both smiled.
Soon the babe was walking
On sturdy well-turned legs
That allowed her to dance and play.
They betrayed her by clumsy falls,
Tears filled and spilled into a cry,
My kisses sought to make it right.
I watched love light her eyes.
The streets and walls changed name and hue,
The babe also changed to grow anew.
She became an artful strong-willed child,

Cornelia Benavidez

Who loved wolves and all things wild.
Imagination embraced, skilled and kind.
A past touched by sadness,
Its shadow marked her frame.
The seasons turned, marking time,
The child bloomed and grew,
Oddly both bold and yet shy.
A women's heart struggled to be born
In the breast of a love-torn child.
I watched the battles in her eyes.
Soon she had a filly's grace,
Pranced strong and hard
With a wind-tossed mane.
She broke out into a full-out run.
The boys gaped their wonder,
They tried but could not keep up.
As she faced both past and present
With a warrior's heart,
Wrestling with both loss and gain.
A girl filled with emotion's pain,
Her mind ruled by ambition,
An ocean of turmoil and star-filled skies.
I watched the courage born in her eyes,
How can she be this young woman full grown?
My child of sweetness and fire born.
Both critique and humor lash from her pen,
A complex woman, not easy to win.
She tests the boundaries of her life,
Soft of lip and sharp of tongue,
Her voice speaks her wisdom.
Lived and trained both hard won.
Athena, Delilah, Persephone, Sappho,
She seeks to test both truth and lie.
Aphrodite and Diana are all her kin
This I always knew, my fierce star child.
I could see it in your eyes.

Hope

March on, children,
You are the courage of the ages.
March on, children,
You are the hope of changes.
You are the product of love and tears unknown.
You are their voices and songs now strong.
March on, children,
Make the world see your love unfurled,
Give the wisdom of ages a new rebirth.

Cornelia Benavidez

Noticing

If I had not paid attention
I would not have noticed
That pinecones do not stand sentry-like
At the tops of towering firs.
My trusty binoculars instead revealed
Nigh dozens of Cedar Waxwings
Watchful of Yamhill's waking.
Are my sleep-encrusted eyes
And early morning stumblings
A threat to their treasure trove
Of luscious elderberries
Awaiting their greedy beaks
And hungry bellies?

If I had not paid attention
I would not have heard,
Over the singing soap opera drama
On the stage of my bird feeder,
The wind flashing through
In the trees like a joyous skateboarder.
Zephyr held out his hand
To tickle my wind chimes
In perfect scale and in harmony.
I muted out all other sound
Threw open my door
To breathe in fresh air and music
The gift of my celestial visitor.

Social Media Thanks

I am thankful for warm smiles
And warmer memories.
I am thankful for kind words
As well as the wicked humor.
I am thankful for all love
That sits at every table.
I am thankful for all hope
Bursting forth like a seed in snow.
I am thankful for all reminders
Of courage, forgiveness and kindness.
I am thankful for the tippy tapping
Of thousands of fingers
That are a Thanks and a Giving
From all our hearts to each other.

Papa

What a strange life you have had,
With all the tales the good and bad.
A sweet boy surrounded by fears,
Hard work and the many tears.
Yet, you found your way
To be a hero in so many ways;
Whether saving a bakery from a blast,
Or saving baby blue jays in their nest,
Picking cotton or weeding fields,
Lifting bales or tending steel.
The questing young man
Who sought a wife.
The spiritual man who gave his life
To God and what he hoped was right.
And to golden and brown-haired curls,
How much you loved your little girls.
You did your best with your art.
But most of all with your loving heart.
I don't think you'll ever know
How much you helped me grow.
Though for long I travelled far away,
Someday soon for you, it will be the same.
Yes, though each other we might miss,
Our love is ever bonded with a daughter's kiss.

Trio Haiku

Words and pictures fly through doorways
    On the computer
    Like freed birds

Thoughts roam or flash through lanes
    Of busy traffic
    Trying to find home

Songs float in universal space
    Like rain from heaven to be drunk by us
    To re-escape from endless faces

Cornelia Benavidez

Remembering Now

Hay monoliths stand bold against the blue late summer sky,
The old oak is defiant in its beauty as it stands guard
Over the fields ripened gold by the sun.
Blackberries hang heavy on the vine,
The air smells sweet with the scent of roses
And catnip flowers to inspire the bees to not despair.
The deer graze with the horses,
As the vulture flies, teasing the wind.
The geese swim content in their pond.
I am the lens and the camera.
I am surrounded by untold eyes.
We are filled with vision and perfect love.

Moment by moment,
In the midst of sadness,
In the midst of loss,
In the midst of chaos,
In the midst of confusion
There is the picture of perfection.
It is the ever-possible gift,
Waiting to be noticed,
Waiting for our care,
Our garden of love,
In this moment of now.

Hay bales near the old farm

Tears Fall Like Rain

Tears fall like rain
When the ache of loss
That tidal wave of darkness
Falls over us a brutal ravishing
We are cold and alone
Left desolate and bleeding
Tears fall like rain

Tears fall like rain
With determined work
The blossom of accomplishment
The fierce joy of rightness
A community of purpose
Awoken and filled
Tears fall like rain

Tears fall like rain
When beauty takes you
Like the pain of first love
Ecstasy's soaring soul
Lifts us to the divine
Embraced and ennobled
Tears fall like rain

Friends

Friendship
The cousin of love
The brother of partnership
The sister of community
The spirit of family

My friends
The flowers in fields of memory
The hands that held mine
Their voices the songs of my life
In their smiles I am home

Eulogy

Victor H. Anderson,
A person born by storm and raised by fire,
The thunderer of the Gods,
The composer of the Goddess.
You who stood on the very shores of Her silver sea,
You who looked upon Her bright and terrible beauty
And dared to heed and hear Her voice.
I salute you, O Victorious.
I salute your spirit of courage,
Your thirst for truth,
Your strength of will,
Your passion for life,
And your unending curiosity.

Master storyteller,
Bard of a hundred tongues,
Man of many ways and names,
You who so generously shared yourself
To all that had the ears to listen.
You were not only my treasure,
You were an international treasure.
The melting pot of the Goddess,
She brought forth Victor Anderson,
Through a great storm,
To be our American Shaman, Priest, Teacher, Friend
And beloved husband of Cora.
Hasta Luego, Blessed be and Aloha.

Poems of Passion and Love

It is thought that in love, poetry has its glory and strongest influence. Though young children might giggle at descriptions of passion or romantic love, preferring their innocent rhymes, here they do come to know that another world awaits them. Later, cynical youth might scoff at poetry's charms while it stirs a deep-down excitement even for them; for there in poetry lies a glimpse of the mysteries of adulthood with its sexual ecstasies and ever-changing future.

Love and passion colors our world for both good and ill. From our obsessions to great achievements, from the pain of longing, be it sexual or spiritual, to the love of our family, friends and pets. We thrill to the birth of awe and wonder of the glorious vistas around our earth that inspires love of the land. The love of creatures all over the earth that also draws forth the love of existence itself. It is then, through the beloved, be it child, lover or spouse, and through our spiritual ideals, that we can fully embrace the most fulfilling satisfactions of life. Be it for Goddess or God or for the consciousness of a whole universe, the fundamental need to express and create life and art is the ultimate act of love. It is through our passion for answers to the mysteries of life that science is born. It is through the passion for expression that the arts are born. It is through our passion and longing for a clean channel to connect to the very source of our soul that all forms of religion are born. The first glimpse of love from another sets our spirit toward the quest that makes us never tire to be here and see this love reflected to us in endless ways. To be separated from love is humanity's greatest sorrow and tragedy, where we must come to battle with the potential seeds of evil itself.

Cornelia Benavidez

For All the Times I Have Loved

I have no regrets
Though at times
Surely
Cupid awoke with malice
And quirky mischief
In his eternal heart

Perhaps
It was not him
I should seek to blame
But curiosity
And loneliness
That fueled idle passions?

Then again, each
That have knocked
Or pounded
On my doorways
Have somehow found
Their way to my heart

I have been left
Bemused
At my passions desire
No regrets.... Yet if
I ever come upon Cupid sleeping
I just might steal his arrows.

Rush

You make me feel
Like a cheetah
On the run

I want to race
Like whitewater horses
Having their fun

Want to play and fly
Like eagles
Diving in the sky

We are bright flames
Entwined lovers
Burning bright

Your Smile

Your smile
A brush stroke
Conveying welcome

Your smile
The flash that
Brightens my world

Your Lips

Your lips are so soft and tender
These lips I'll always remember
Lips just like a child
Lips like a teasing girl
Lips with a vampire thrill
Lips with a poet's art
Yet still with a man's heart

Looking Back

I wish that I could tell you
All the times that I miss;
From lovely conversations
To the rare tender kiss.

I wish that I could tell you
How memories make me smile;
From the silly quarrels
To the keenness of your mind.

I wish that I could tell you
I miss your voice and healing hands;
The way you held your cigarette
It's the sweetest hurt with no regrets.

Night Watch

The night has been restless.
I have been pacing,
Considering and weighing,
Like a coin rubbed
Gently turned over and over.
For many months
The faint shadow of you,
Like Peter Pan hung everywhere.
I catch a glimpse here and there:
A glimmer of hope, a tide of sorrow.
The clock pushes with the full moon,
The midyear is upon us.
A foal has been born,
While a robin tests its baby wings.
Life stirs amidst the shadows.
Your eyes are robin egg blue,
But it is in the eyes of the stallion
That I see your complex heart.
I have been searching for words,
A weary prospector for meaningful gold.
How did I know that now is not our time
And that you need arms much stronger than mine?
Can I let you grieve and say this is wise?
I walk among the trees,
Dream of the space between the stars.
Will the horse run free to claim his soul?
Can he see all the love that lets him go?
And that near or far I bless him so,
Watching, waiting, expecting the dawn.
I have been wondering at this love,
Sister, friend, brother, lover,
The vision quest and the inner battles
Refuse to be a saddle and yes, love always matters.

A wondrous rose that gifted me with its presence to inspire me

Cornelia Benavidez

The Rose

The rose as she first appeared
Was golden in hue,
A shy pink at her stem,
A promise of a gentle bloom.
And when the Sun's fire caressed
And kissed this pale shade,
It unveiled and opened.
With pride and trust
Of all her heart was made,
Pink deepened to a rosy red.
She bloomed to passion's fire
and turned velvet in her desire,
Red like wine, red like blood.
Her heady scent filled with life,
Longing for rain, waiting for love.
Yet, the sun became a brutal lover,
Faulting the rose for her softness,
Her need for his light, her need for water.
Sadly she hung her head.
With a dancer's grace a petal fell.
I think I am dying of a broken heart, thought she.
Nay, it is of another's careless touch, said he.
It was at first a chilling thrill:
The thunder roared, the water spilled.
Lighting flashed, the sky it is neon lit,
A beauteous rose is water kissed.
So when the sun next saw his lover,
She was filled with water's joy, not sorrow.
And though the storm had lost its power,
The rose was no more a lonely flower.

Cornelia Benavidez

Yes, I Will Love You Forever, But...

If you ignore me again
This time
I shall not be so kind

If you run away again
Like a justified, petulant child
I shall not turn the other eye

If you hurt me again
This time
I shall not let it lie

Do not betray me again
I mean not in foolish ways
But in the daggers of words

Do not toy with me again
For the thread of time
Knows our bond and will judge

Do not make me watch
As you make the same mistakes
When you have been blessed

This is not the time
For cowboy thrills
Or martyred princes

This is a time to shine
Your light and love on your work
The hope of the divine soul

The Moment

A moment
A moment of shared warmth
A moment of understanding
A moment of sadness
A moment before good-bye

Persistence

You stand there with your half-meant smile,
Panther in your voice and in your hard-dark eyes,
While telling me all the reasons why:
Like why you can't be happy,
Why life is so hard,
Why you have no patience,
Yet how in control you are.
So, I find myself like a ball of yarn,
Soft and round and all caught up,
Like a moth to a flame,
Like a serpent charmed.
I'll fan the embers I won't give up,
Gotta be cool and clear and so precise,
Wondering why I have to be so crucified.
Now here we are holding our telephones,
It's a weapon of distance and it's so alone.
You spit like a viper through the telephone line,
I swallowed the poison and barely survived.
Oh, baby, you can't be no devil,
And I'm no Madonna's child.
Don't let what we had completely die.
Let's have the best of us survive,
What's deep and true in you and in I.

Cornelia Benavidez

Wild Heart

There's guesswork on the news lines
Washed over many hands
Interrupters of veiled illusions
While we dance to their plans
I avenge myself, pen in hand
I may not change the world
But it will know where I stand.
There is such an empty sorrow
In your soulful eyes
Full of such good intentions
And your practiced righteous lies
I have struggled for my soul
And it has left its mark.
You may fear my words
But you can trust my heart
No, sweet love, it's never easy
When you're stumbling in the dark
It's the hard way to find out
That scorpions hide under rocks.
There's too many convoluted ways
Of hiding from yourself
You so want a little heaven
But you give yourself hell.
I see it in you,
Have felt it in myself
We live, and we die
By what we sell
A cry goes up
In the wildness of my heart
A prayer offered up
To give wings to this art
Let the spirit of creation
Sing out all doubt.

Shut down

There is a place
There is a cave
In a women's heart
Where all is quiet
Safe and cool with love
There is room for:

The view of memories
For an adequate hearth
A large dog to guard
The wide entrance
And a few good cats
That will guard her soul.

Little Isis and I having a moment

Cornelia Benavidez

The Gypsy and the Gaul

For now, I'll tell you a story,
And yes, you'll know it's true,
Of a gypsy girl and her lover
With his eyes of turquoise blue.

Her skin was fair as moonlight,
Her hair a long stormy cloud,
Her lips burned with songs like fire,
Her mysteries in eyes deep brown.

He first saw her like a shadow,
A laughing, dancing teasing dream.
She saw him kind and gentle,
In his eyes, the sparkling seas.

Deep in a greenwood forest,
They met one day in spring.
Tender passion filled the hours,
Now her finger bore a ring.

Then one day when autumn fell,
She knew that he was gone.
In desperate hope, she sought the home
Of the old crone sung of by the bards.

'Old woman I have an empty heart
That only one man can fill.
Tomorrow is the day of hearts,
Gold coins for a true love spell.'

She was waiting by the river bank,
When his shadow cross her fell.
She turned to him in joy and sorrow,
The spell had worked right well.

Why have you summoned me, my love?
When I build you a great surprise?
A castle for my gypsy princess,
Laughed his turquoise eyes.

The Sweetness That is in You

It is more than the twinkle in your eyes.
It is more than the humor or poetic lines:
It is in the core of your Irish name
That ties you to Gods of ancient fame,
Both the warrior and gentle dove,
The bullish man I had grown to love,

The Long Poem

Storytelling Through Poetry

We have poems that can speak of anything, or anyone, and that can address any emotion or philosophical thought. Still, it is the long poem that may convey itself as an essay in verse. One type can present itself as an explosive political rant that can stand on its own. Others might become philosophical spoken word accompanied by a drum beat or other various instrumentation. This has been with us in modern times since the Beatnik poets. Now we have what the young call slam poetry; the laying down of poetry on the table so-to-speak and, afterwards, the drop of the mike, the walk away. This finish says I have spoken. It is the 'this is the how it is done' move of many young poet performers today.

The long story poem is also storytelling in verse and rhyme; it might be an amusing tale for adults or for children. Often it carries themes of mystery, adventure or humor that are pushed to their conclusion by the rhyme and rhythm of the words in the verse. This adds to the excitement of the telling of the tale, especially in a performance setting. This type of poem, for me, has always worked best for the telling of a romantic, fairy-tale type piece, or a poem that has a teasing tone or even a scary one. The story 'The Home' was inspired by an old hospital that was shut down and then reopened as an old folk's home (as they called them back in the day in my Michigan home town of Albion). We children heard, and passed about, tales about this old hospital; that it was filled with the ghosts of people long gone from the 1800s, who greeted those that now were waiting to pass. I happened to think on the old hospital and this scary, yet humorous story came to mind.

Cornelia Benavidez

The Home

The Home stood next to the cemetery,
Cold brown stone next to colder gray stone.
The place held the heaviness of waiting
And the hidden ticking of time.

Please push the buzzer,
It said at the door.
A cool may I help you?
I am here for the tour.

She had answered the ad,
Had the interview by phone.
She was the only one who said
She was not afraid to be alone.

The girl blinked to the dimness,
Though the door was held wide.
So, good of you to come this late
As they headed to an oasis of light.

They greeted a man with very white teeth.
We'll start right away this way please.
Her feet softly tapped the polished floor.
He led the way to another door.

Ours is a proud old institution,
Been here since eighteen O eight.
It was a prison of sorts,
Back in those good old days.

It was just social deviates
All thrown in together.
That's all changed of course,
In modern times, it got better.

The jingle of too many keys,
 A door of metal and heavy hardwood.
This is for their protection, he says,
With the smile that points it's understood.

The sound of a TV playing game shows,
Old men playing checkers, keeping score.
Little old ladies dressed like pretty pink violets.
Orderlies and Nurses with lists and assignments.

Tomorrow starts the long weekend.
They should sleep through to the day.
The staff will see to all medication.
Of course, for some it's a Holiday.

Cornelia Benavidez

Here is the office with numbers you need.
Here are flashlights and the hidden keys,
In every wing, anything you might need:
Extra diapers, towels and the cat's feed.

This is only for one night, only eleven hours.
The staff will return by eight on the morrow.
Any questions? he asked, with a tilted head.
I will be here all alone? the young girl asked.

There will be security cams on the outer grounds.
He flashed a smile: Let's finish our rounds.
You have the number of the man at the outer gate.
Like the ad said, it's just a one-night date.

They took a peek from bed to bed.
They glided through room to room,
To those that spoke, to those near dead.
She fought the tingle of a chilly gloom.

Then, just as if reading her mood:
Natural to feel a little sad, he soothed,
Also, I hope that no rumors you've heard,
Of haunted tales and ghostly words.

When he finally left with his last frozen smile,
He had worked her nerves she realized.
Yet all seemed calm and strangely quiet.
An unease tickled her mind, but she defied it.

Yet as her feet tipped back toward the office,
One by one each ceiling light went out.
The darkness stretched, a long dark funnel,
With a distant light at the end of the tunnel.

She took a deep breath, walking once more,
Following the small lights on the floor.
As her eyes adjusted to the soft dimness,
She was grateful for her wits and fitness.

In the office, she reached eagerly for the flashlight,
Checked that it worked and was satisfied.
Still she bumped the desk and bruised her hip.
She rubbed the spot and bit her lip.

A light on the clock revealed 10:10.
I better do my rounds, she said in her head.
Just follow the signs and the lights on the floor.
I should not get lost – under her breath she swore.

On her way, she found the cafeteria,
Made herself a little snack,
Carried it to a little table.
Did she hear a scritch, scritch scratch?

Oh, great they must have mice or rats
In this old place. Wouldn't surprise me a bit.
Her hasty-made food down she gobbled.
At the edge of the dark did she hear a shuffle?

She shone the flashlight through the dark,
Hoping that it would light the mark.
Yet nothing was there or seemed amiss.
Shrugged her shoulders, put away her dish.

Now I should make my first bed check.
Hopefully all will be well, aloud she said.
These halls have such a spooky hollow.
If I keep busy, soon it will be tomorrow.

Cornelia Benavidez

Not wishing to invade or disturb,
She poked only her head at each door.
Some breathed softly or loudly snored.
Some lay huddled and fully covered.

As she made her way back toward the office,
She went to a window and looked outside.
The moon now shone so full, big and bright.
The front gate seemed so far away at night.

She took a deep breath, let out a sigh.
Somehow, she knew it would be a long night.
She made her way down the corridor.
When all went dark, no lights on the floor.

Now what is this? she said out loud.
Darkness now swept like a long dark shroud.
There in its depths, voices whispered and cooed.
All her hairs raised, fearing some doom.

Who are you! Who are you! She did shout.
Do you know why the lights went out?
But silence answered back like a scream.
Now she felt trapped in some bad dream.

Brandishing the flashlight like a sword,
With shaking knees, she ran for the next door.
The voices now whispered like some bad tune,
And they were saying: too soon, too soon.

She did her best to run on the polished floor,
Finding her way, her hip still sore.
Yet slip she did, slid hard into a heap.
White icy hands from the shadows did reach.

She tried to scream, her breath was knocked out.
She could not move, could not shout.
She was gently lifted to ghastly faces.
A hand to her face and soon she fainted.

She awoke feeling ill in total darkness
And thought of her purse and cell in the office.
She felt about and found a tiny flashlight.
She was in an empty storeroom all locked tight.

She searched all about, found only a bottle of water
With a little note that said: relax soon it will be over.
With the tiny light, she searched everywhere.
As the little light dimmed her tears overwhelmed.

It seemed like forever, she prayed, and cried,
When noise she heard on the door's other side.
A sweet little voice all full of concern:
Where are you, my dear! Are you alright?

Please help! I'm here! she cried and pounded.
The door then opened and to her astounding,
She fell into the arms of a host of strange creatures:
Goblins, zombies, werewolves and witches.

Quick! said a voice, lay her down on the gurney.
Oh, the dear sweet thing, she is so pretty.
Wheel her to the small waiting room.
We must be quick for the sun does loom.

A new terror now in her heart grew.
She wanted to struggle yet still too weak to move.
They did their best to lift her onto a couch.
They brought her a blanket and gathered about.

Cornelia Benavidez

They mumbled softly as they patted her hand,
When the lady said: we better remove our masks.
There underneath each monstrous face,
An old wrinkled visage took its place.

They then helped her sit up, a cool cloth to her head,
And the glass of juice placed in her shaking hands.
You will be all right, we are so sorry dear.
This is not how it goes and not what we planned.

So, we shall tell you the story, so you understand,
And hope you not hate us for the night you have had.
We are the weak, abandoned, old and alone.
We have only each other and this is our home.

Yes, for the most part they all mean well.
Sometimes it's for safety, still sometimes it's hell.
Yet we all work hard for our one day a year,
When we taste again freedom with nothing to fear.

This is the tradition for a long time.
It's very well planned every minute of time,
But Will got wacky, pulled the plug too soon
You saw not the milk and cookies in the room.

You would have then gone to a gentle sleep,
Woke on the morrow with nothing to fear,
While we had our fun till sun's first light,
No one ever knows us on Halloween night.

So here is your purse, dear, and some food.
We wish you no ill, hope that's understood,
And for all your fright, here are some extra bills.
We hope it will help you to bear no ill will.

She drank her juice and was feeling better.
A part of her wanted to yell and cuss,
Yet the bigger part wanted to laugh out loud.
Please give me space, please don't fuss.

This is all very crazy, still I sort of understand.
Yet could end tragic no matter how well planned.
You say that this has been happening for a long spell.
Who had this idea, so it could work long so well?

Well that, dear, is quite a story that is true.
We have a friend who helps us through.
He never had the chance to escape,
So he makes sure we have our date.

So as this old woman told these words,
A strange light in the room twirled.
It raised the girl's hackles; her eyes grew wide,
As a ghostly form stood by their sides.

He took a bow
After a little spin,
Gave her a wink
With a cheeky grin.

The food and bills they did fly,
She grabbed her purse in the blink of an eye.
As the costumed oldsters watched her run away,
Oh dear, said the lady, another who cannot stay.

Still, we have had our sweet Hallows night
Let us be in our beds with the coming light.
So, fret you not and never fear
We will be ready... for the next year.

Poems of Humor and Whimsy

Children delight in the power of humor, especially in rhyme. Humor is a pulse of life, the beat of hope as it invokes laughter and teases all of us to consider the implications between the lines. It is a place where wisdom finds safety in wit and fantasy. Here, in the written or spoken word, humankind can pause and, with a lightened heart, readdress deep fears and pain, perhaps finding new perspectives and even forgiveness. In humor, romance finds balance and anger finds reason. Humor teaches not just children, but adults as well, to think outside of our boxes, to reconsider the possibilities, or at least to be charmed by the whimsy. Silliness and even the ironic, fires a kind of reassurance of our connection to others and that our imaginations somehow connect and flow out of this Divine healing force.

Humor and whimsy are reflected all through the universe, for do we not see them everywhere in nature? How can we not laugh when we see a platypus, or marvel at a huge bird, like the ostrich, which cannot fly? Or when we confront the gangly beauty of a giraffe or the strange powerful grace of a rhino? These oddities are also all through our oceans, and even in the far reaches of space we see galaxies shaped like seahorses, or a huge, peering, truly cosmic eye. Here too, we find connection to the mysterious that helps to guide and cheer us when we feel so ignorant and ungraceful, allowing us at times to stumble into greater truths.

Does the universe laugh at us or with us? Perhaps, it is both, if our consciousness and that of the divine truly reflect each other.

Cornelia Benavidez

Silly Musings

First, we learn about how to float,
Then we learn how to build the boat.
We learn to move and not to flounder,
And finally, how to float for longer.
In between we slip and slide,
Sometimes fall, sometimes glide.
All in all, we gain our stride,
And with a little luck, we finally fly.
Thus, does the piper become the pied

The Cowboy
and the Greenhorn Gal

Oh, to conquer the Western male
If you can catch him
Between cows and jail.

Oh, the powers of a tenderfoot
If she has long curls
And a smile to boot.

She was wanting a horse to ride.
He strides to the corral
With manly pride.

So she says, 'I'm a little green.'
He wonders if she knows
What that really means.

On the biggest horse
She will ride
Straight up the mountainside.

I will see if she has horse sense
By whether or not
she breaks her neck.

Oh, the courage of the Eastern girl
As she held on so tight
Closed her eyes to the peril.

Cornelia Benavidez

She rode with ladylike grace
Full knowing tomorrow
The price she must face.

And though her gentle charms would never show
That tenderfoot she is no more.
One Cowboy knows just how sweet and saddle sore.

Linda on her beloved Leggs

The Beauty of Morning

I open the door
To sunlight's early kiss
Gentle on my skin
Before its midday nip.

I step to the porch
The early birds chatter
Diving and chirping
Joyful for my clatter.

Food for the chickens
Wild birds galore
Food for the kitties
The geese and the dogs.

Water tomatoes and
The critters and roses
Gather the eggs
Pet the horses' noses.

Do I put on the kettle?
What shall I do instead?
The answer is easy
Go back to bed.

Cornelia Benavidez

A Ditty for You, Dear

Yes, I will admit it's true
That only Newman had eyes as blue,
And no one could beat that wily grin
Or tempt a heart to want to sin,
Still make my heart go pitter pat,
Make my body want to melt.
But it does not matter what I felt
I am lookin' for you in someone else.

You put my mind in a fog,
You slimy greasy old hotdog.
Don't you dare walk away,
I've still got some things left to say/
And don't you dare call me sister,
My knuckles comin' for your kisser.
Hope I knock you some good horse sense,
Cuz I'll be lookin' for you in someone else.

Yes, you hurt me. That is a fact
You silly, dirty old sewer rat.
And yes, I will admit it's true
That you never did say I love you.
You have my heart, that you sighed,
And now you say that you lied?
I'll miss your goods, that's what you said?
Oh, I'm so lookin' for you in someone else.

Modern Life

There comes a time in everyone's life
When you feel you're more than a little insane.
All the everyday stresses not to mention
Your personal everyday little messes
Are almost enough to blow out your brains.
You need a little comfort.
You need a little sleep.
You need a little peace.
Yet you're lucky if you can click
With someone a good stiff drink.
So, you'll try some meditation,
Hoping for some alleviation.
You will check out Jesus, Buddha and Yoda:
They all have their ways to atone ya.
Be it Kid Rock or good old Dylan,
They all will have their opinion.
So, here, is what I have to say:

Lord save me from the milk toast people,
From all the ones that even mean so well.
Thank you for all my brilliant crazies,
Even when they make life a little hell.
Save us all from the righteously inane.
You gain so much from the creatively insane.
So, give me the moody artist,
A colorful sassy little bitch,
The brilliant writer with an itch.
They may be difficult and goring,
Yet never will they be boring.
And yes, they are all out to get ya.
Yes, you are right my dear ole Ma.
So, no matter how others depress

Cornelia Benavidez

Freak you out or oppress,
Be it here or in the hereafter,
Somehow it all does matter,
And somehow it will all make sense,
All this beauty and craziness.

So, befriend a crazy friend or two
Believe in all the good Karma for you.
Never forget this grace so rare,
As you will say this little prayer:
Lord save me from the milk toast people,
Who want your soul to never give it back.
Let me appreciate the poetically surly,
The deep voiced colorful girlie.
I will give you love, just give me passion,
And please a good sense of fashion.
May I not be a complete doormat,
And not too thin or too fat.
Though friends might roll their eyes and sigh
At least I do sleep well at night.

Little Girl Limerick

There was a girl that could smile
She also could walk a mile
But two she couldn't,
She just wouldn't do it
So, she sat down to rest for a while

Critters

Dreamland, such a sweet repose
Cannot resist a cold wet nose
Doggie breath and warm wet tongue
You try to hide yet nowhere to run
Just when you think you've won five minutes
Each morning you still resist this
As geese honk loud with rooster crows
Next comes the dancing kneading kitty paws
With pointy claws and sweet meow meows
Outside the window sing sparrows and finches
You moan and groan as this all pinches
A cup of coffee and one big yawn
You bravely face another critter dawn.

Cornelia Benavidez

The Fairy and the Bee

Please tell me your secret,
Said the fairy to the bee.
Why does your honey taste so sweet?
Before you fly
Do you dance a spell?
Is it found in the clover's smell?

Now you listen. strawberry top,
To be busy is our lot.
Honey is the gift we give
From the flowers that you tend.
Our secret is as old as time to mind
And only for a bee to find.

Swift Encounter

Determined and seeking
She climbed her way
Through the flowers and thorns
On a mild windy day
Come now, really? As you ask why
So gentle a creature on a blackberry find
Sweetly singing joyous and wise
The twinkling of the stars in her eyes
A charming young fairy
A hundred years shy
She smiles at you softly
As she pauses at her play
You blink your eyes
And she flashes away
As a butterfly song escapes her lips
And fills you up like a lover's kiss

Gnomes

Between spaces are worlds unknown
There lies the place of little gnomes
Fierce yet kind
Humorous and wise
Let's hear it for these little guys
Who do so much no matter their size.
They are the guardians of shrooms and plants
Love to tweak the tails of all the cats
And whisper in the doggies' ears
Of mischief, rabbits and the running deer.
Here and there we may peek
At their world we ever seek
Yet to see we must be as a child
Fierce, sweet, innocent and wild.

Flirt

He is cool as a dewdrop morning
As sweet as summer rain
He flashes like a firefly
Then runs away again

Childlike and bittersweet wise
Yet free as tousled hair
Warm passion in his eyes
A smile of innocent air.

He brings you a taste of Fairyland
Though your fingers may catch a sting
Peeking from the shadows and
His light laughter on the wind.

Do you think that you can see him?
Do you think you know his name?
He is the son of magic
It's love running in his veins.

Pomp and Circumstance

A King may have his golden crown
Perched high upon his noble brow.
He may have a hundred horses,
Jewels and lands from many sources,
A populace both rich and fat,
While on oak and gold, the judges sat.
Yet it matters not a twit,
In the eyes of his government,
Without pomp and circumstance.

Even sitting on his throne,
A King must stand alone.
He does have his trusty charger
And a suit of golden armor;
All that makes such a nice romance,
All surveyed with a royal glance.
Yet it matters not a hoot:
He can still get the preverbal boot
Without pomp and circumstance.

Ah the burdens of the high and mighty,
Such is the weight of a golden crown.
You must not take that glory lightly,
While still politely hold your ground.
Please pretend it all goes smoothly,
Never say that you can fool me,
And never say what you meant,
Be it from the crass to the elegant
Without pomp and circumstance.

Cornelia Benavidez

A King's conscience must be level,
Though his hand may shake the devil's.
The job must bravely be done,
Speeches and wars are to be won.
And the price we pay for this fun,
As the treasury becomes all undone,
The public's pockets they'll be empty,
Yet still they will cheer you greatly,
If you have the pomp and circumstance.

The Epic poem

Passing History and Myth into the Future

In history, our greatest heroes, be they gods or men, told the tales of the people. Here, a tribe's creation and emerging identity found its shape. The epic poem is most likely the descendent of oral tradition and elemental performance, the chants and tales that impress upon their listeners the lessons of tribal history and recount the grace, as well as the vengeance, of gods and men. It is the journey of courage for the hero and heroine that created the romance of the beloved. Their journey pleases not only us it seems, but the forces of fate and even the gods themselves. The epic poem may relate tribal myth and lore as much as it does individual accomplishments, or it might reveal a mystery or a fundamental truth of human existence. It can also be inspired by the dreams and visions of shamans and elders. The epic tale usually offers both hope and warnings of the consequences of action without thought, or the results of passion that inspire the hero to victory or tragedy, sometimes both. It may also offer explanations of why such things have come to pass.

The following is a story that I turned into an epic poem. It was told to me long ago in San Francisco. I'd met a young black man whose family had long lived in the Caribbean, yet they still carried with them tales and lore from their African past. One of those traditions was the telling through the purple veil. This meant that the story about to be told was of special and sacred significance. The audience or listener sat on one side of a large purple cloth hung from the ceiling and the storyteller sat on the other side. Most of the time, the teller just spoke, but sometimes for special occasions, or for children, he or she might light candles to display hand movements in the shadows on the cloth. I am sure that sometimes, under various situations, the purple veil needed to be imagined, but the meaning was still clear: That the telling of this story was as a sacred rite.

We did not have a purple cloth, so this young man told me to relax and close my eyes as he sat down on my white rug in Project One, the artist colony I was living in at the time. He then unveiled for me this amazing story. After he was done, he bid me to hold the tale in my heart and to only repeat it to people who would value it. The tale was then to be told only privately, unless I felt it was ready to be revealed, and even then, carefully. He said that there were few left that knew the story as he did, and he was not sure if he would be able to pass the story on, as his grandfather did to his mother and all his ancestors before them. For some reason, he felt very moved to tell me the tale. In keeping with my promise, because I am not of this young man's family tradition, I have taken the spirit of this epic story as best as I can remember and turned it into a poem to share with you. I believe that the time for sharing the mysteries of our past has come, and this includes the legends of the Nephilim.

Nephilim
Part I

Come and listen, sons and daughters!
Sit behind the purpled veil,
As I tell this ancient tale.
It is of Gods' and Heroes', quests.
Hold thy children to thy breast.
We have whispered it for centuries,
From Priest to King to Priest.
Hear it as I tell you, sitting at my feet.

Our Priestess can tell the tale by song and dance,
This ancient mystery from our past.
As leaping fires call out toward the stars,
Quiet your mind and open your heart,
For this is a tale both true and sacred
It is a truth both bold and naked.
Tell it not to foolish ears or the hardened soul,
So, you may grow bountiful and old.

Cornelia Benavidez

It was ancient in my father's father's time,
And will be more so in your children's children.
This sacred tale of Gods and men,
When all of nature was our kindred friend.
We lived in peace in caves near a river,
In long-ago times not easily remembered,
Far over the mountains and other tribes
Who wanted not what is yours and mine.

We watched the sky for omens and signs.
We wondered at all the mysteries,
By sun and moon, cloud and star.
We told our tales against the dark,
And the gifts of the Goddesses' love,
Trusting the signs from high above.
The elders sang the songs of our making
With our innocence never breaking.

They say one night the sky burned
With a thunder, our world trembled and turned.
Our ancestors thought the moon had shattered,
As when dying stars like petals scatter,
We all hid like a tribe of frightened deer,
Even the bravest of our warriors was a-feared,
Before emerging from caves to wonder
What God had ripped our earth asunder.

The warriors and elders bravely went to find
What message the Gods might have left behind?
They saw a trail of smoke in the sky.
They followed it to hear a strange sigh.
There splitting the ground a giant shining stone:
Was this a part fallen from the moon?
They now saw in the air a smaller flying rock.
Their fear was so great their hearts almost stopped.

Was this a battle of Moon and Sun?
Who had lost and who had won?
Or is this somehow a visitation?
We did not give or ask such invitation.
Is this of the Gods to some great purpose,
Or some demon come to hurt us?
Or have we done some great offense?
They crept from this sight to consider this.

We gathered at our hallowed caves
That long have sheltered and kept us safe
From the plundering lusts of other men.
Now a great long silence on us fell.
We huddled close in our fear and shock,
Not one spoke to cheer or mock.
'We must drink and eat, break this spell'
Commanded the wise women to think again.

The Elder rose to say, 'Yes, this is wise.
Then we will counsel and divine
Why this fearful mystery has come to us?
For we must have knowledge to decide.
Water we have aplenty and a few dried goods,
Sharing simple things will lift the heavy mood.
Now, wise woman, gather well thy bones
Let us chant and the women moan.'

Gathered in a circle chanting soft and true,
With each beat hope now sprung anew.
The flames flickered in their priestess' eyes,
What she now came to say was a surprise;
'This is not the God's anger, message or mirth,
Nor the sun and moon falling to earth.
It is a fearful power from the skies above.
Let us be wary if these be stranger Gods.'

'This is good counsel,' said the elder father,
'From the spirits and lips of our priestess mother.
Now my daughter will voice her stand,
Heed these words every women and man!'
She then rose like a flower up among them,
Already songs were made to her even then.
Fairest of the fair and taller than some men
Beloved child of the Elder and Wise woman there.

'A few must spy upon the valley,' said she,
'Be as wise as wolves so none may lead.
We must act as if there be a siege,
It matters not what Gods these might be.
Somehow, we must be brave and find out
What these demons or Gods might want.
No matter how fearful, we must not flee.'
Said the young Princess Priestess, the wise Ahnee.

Slowly the sun rose, bathing the valley floor,
The men there long before the sun rose.
They gazed with wonder at the great stone below.
No other flying thing like eagles soared,
So, they nestled in the mountainside.
Each prayed to themselves they would not be spied.
A great unknown fear, yet courage they did not lack.
Just past the high sun, like an egg the stone cracked.

They emerged from this Firebird egg so large,
Now there was no question that these were Gods.
Some were almost the height of two grown men.
They seemed like living trees to them.
To the surprise and wonder of the huddled friends,
The wandering Gods returned to their stone egg again.
Very careful they crawled and then they raced
Running back to the cave at lightening pace.

'Elder wise ones, brothers and sisters, this is what comes!
The flaming Firestone opened, bringing forth giant Gods.
They moved about just as men walking in the sun.
They returned to their egg, making it whole and one.
Is this not wondrous, what can this mean?
The firebird, the thunder and all that has been?'
The Elder rose. 'What say my wife and daughter, Ahnee?
Is this a time to humbly fall on our knees?'

The wise woman rose with a serious thoughtful face.
'Ahnee, come stand by me, take your rightful place.
As you know, our Gods speak to us, this is our art.
These last two days sit heavy on my heart,
Yet nothing of this visitation was revealed to us,
Tho' my dreams have been fitful and restless.
We must take these next days to ponder on this well.
What say you, Ahnee, to the tribe's commonwealth?'

'Beloved Mother and Father and all my kindred!
I have cried out for guidance if we must make amends.
I have searched my dreams, cast the bones and lots,
In us there seems to be no blame or fault.
It seems that these indeed might be Stranger Gods.
If this is so, what might such Gods want?
How can such a thing be and even come to pass?'
All nodded their heads, for how could one guess?

The Elder and his wise women stood again.
'This may be an honor, or this may be a test!
They have not yet even reached out to us.
Our priestess has received no warning or request.
If these are visiting Gods, then they are our God's guests.
Perhaps this is a changing time that only the Gods know,
Or this is our testing and learning time, so we may grow.
Pray, make offerings for the sake our Gods and us below.'

Cornelia Benavidez

So, it was done, dear children, by these brave elder ones
Whose blood flows in your body
and whose spirit shares our hearts.
They watched, prayed and gathered food like silent mice,
Praying for an answer and praying for a sign.
And an answer did come from our Gods to inspire
Of what was to follow and what the Gods might require.
How can we know this? What did the tribe see?
Most of what we know comes from the lips of Ahnee.

The sun rose and set six times and now rose anew,
When from the mountains the great horns blew.
From down the paths came a respectful procession,
Holding aloft food, flowers and other earth treasures,
While the sun rose pink and golden, filling the valley.
Bravely they marched as the Gods did rally.
Two men carried between them a giant spear,
Then they stepped aside to let Ahnee come near.

Her voice rang out, clear, strong and true,
'Gods of Gods we bring our gifts to you!
We made a great spear to match your great height.
We are so honored to witness your great might.
We welcome you to our lives and land,
What more can we offer, what have you planned?'
With this humble call, all dropped to one knee
And bowed their heads with their princess, Ahnee.

The great Egg cracked with a soft hissing sound.
More Gods came forth stepping on the ground.
Heavy steps, then silence like a long-held breath.
Ahnee slowly with grace raised her head.
There they were, a moment too sublime,
The human woman and a God eye to eye.
Slowly He nodded and raised His hand.
Ahnee just as slowly came to a stand.

A deep melodious hum came from His chest.
So, the rest of the people raised their heads.
He pointed to the men who held the spear.
He bid them to approach to him, come near.
The spear was then held up to the great Lord:
'We hope this pleases the Gods that soar.'
The God smiled down to the beauteous girl,
Her eyes deep green, her long dark curls.

The God then held the spear with surprise,
It was well-weighted and matched his great size.
The God's armor shone like the sun from toe to head,
With a deep shout, 'Nimrod!' he said.
Now there stepped forth another God.
He seemed a bit younger and almost as tall.
He took off his headpiece shook his great fair locks.
His face broke into a smile that did not mock.

His eyes leapt like lapis stars from his radiant face.
His shining broad smile was for Ahnee's sake.
A fault in His beauty could none find on him,
Strong like a great lion. What would be his will?
'My brother thanks you for your gift.'
Each brother gave a hand the great spear to lift.
Though the words were not understood,
The meaning was clear, and it rang true.

The Gods then nodded, bid them all to go home.
Ahnee spoke, 'The Gods wish to be alone.'
All the people walked home in silence
And, once there, gathered about the fire.
The children came and nestled close,
As Ahnee the story of this meeting told.
It burned into the hearts of the young and old.
What would now happen? What would unfold?

Nephilim
Part II

And now dear children, and all ears that hear,
Stretch your limbs, then gather back near.
For now, the tale grows ever more complex,
Every heart of both God and man will meet its test.
The names and the places with all their lessons,
The wonder and joy from all that bless us.
Be humble in spirit and all will be well,
This is our story to remember and tell.

The sun rose and set three days.
The people calmly went about their ways,
When from far away a loud sound came.
'This seems to be a call,' said the elder.
'Another meeting with the Gods.
Perhaps now, since all has gone well,
They will now say what they intend,
If they may stay or if they will go?'

The people watched from the high cliff rocks,
While once more Ahnee and the men went down.
Four Gods gathered, the tallest held the spear.
Slowly our people gathered near.
They then were about to do a great bow,
When the one called Nimrod pointed to the ground.
There were markings in the sand.
The tallest God placed his hand on his chest.

'I am Setta,' the deep voice intoned.
'SETTA!' he said more loudly, slapping his breast.
'Nimrod!' he pointed to his brother there.

'Now…' a hand he extended as his great voice asked,
'And now brave woman, what of thee?'
She stepped forward and said, 'Ahnee.'
And she too placed her hand to her chest,
In that moment each knew what the other meant.

Now he pointed to the pictures in the sand,
She could see their river and canyon there.
He pointed to the green stones around her neck.
She smiled and understood what this too meant.
It is not to question the needs and deeds Gods send.
She called over a young man, showed him the map.
'Here is the river and they need the pool of stones,
You will show them where they need to go.'

The one called Nimrod followed the youth,
Whose heart beat with excitement and pride.
His nimble feet stayed ahead of the God's stride,
Up over rocks and down to a canyon bed.
There was the water that ran swift and strong,
Over roots and rocks, little inlets wound.
Nimrod scooped the river bed in his hand,
Smooth green stones lay in a bed of golden sand.

The next day was filled with dark and heavy clouds,
Ahnee and her mother left offerings by a smooth mound.
'No matter what happens we must abide by our ways!'
'Yes, Mother, we must be cautious these days.
Our Gods are everywhere, in every nook of the earth,
They also live in the waters both fresh and salt.'
'These Gods are powerful and strong,
They are of Air and Fire,' her mother warned.

The heavy rain kept everyone home for two days,
The tribe tended to craft and children in the caves.
The sun rose on rain like jewels scattered over the land.

191

Cornelia Benavidez

Ahnee caught her breath as she spied a tall man,
Nimrod, who was standing at a respectful distance.
Slowly and solemnly she walked up toward him.
Gracefully she bowed to one knee, palms up in greeting,
Waiting for his word to arise and why this meeting.

Instead Nimrod grabbed the tree limb over them,
Giving a mighty shake the cool rain-bowed drops fell,
Showered upon Ahnee,
Who gasped with the smallest screech.
He offered his mighty hand to bring her to her feet,
With a warm heartfelt laugh to ease her nerves.
Drops of water sparkled in her hair, raced about her curves.
He pointed behind him to sitting places covered by cloth
And food on shining plates, she knew not of what.

She was being asked to break food with a God!
She was a little frightened and a bit overcome,
Yet when she dared glance up to his face, his eyes spoke.
There was kindness, curiosity, even humor in his look
As he poured a drink in a fine bowl with a holding stick,
Then put food on a small but heavy platter and bid her to eat.
He showed her tools for eating the food
To make her head spin.
She had no idea he thought her a wonder,
As much she did him.

Ahnee sat quietly, eating slowly and carefully,
While Nimrod crushed food in his great teeth,
All the while watching her from his seat.
With tools he scooped up what he needed
That with Ahnee knew not how to eat.
He fed her as a child. She felt embarrassed,
Yet her shy smile gave him pleasure
In this moment of peace and leisure.

He poured water in a goblet hard as stone,
Like the sun, it gleamed and shone.
From this wonder, he did sip,
Then gently pressed the goblet to her lips.
The sharing of water was a rite of friendship,
Yet when shared with the Gods is like a marriage.
Her inner mind laughed at such a thought,
As she dared not assume what the God sought.

Nimrod then took his long staff.
With it he began to draw upon the sand.
He drew the outline of her caves there.
He drew little people and one with long hair.
He pointed to it and then to Ahnee,
Who blushed and placed her hand to breast.
He nodded, and then they both laughed,
As the wind danced the leaves above their heads.

He then drew a tall figure and said, 'Sister Suala,'
Then drew another with a tall spear and said, 'Brother Setta.'
He drew behind them a high smooth cliffside.
Then drew a very tall opening in its side.
He erased the opening and pointed to the cliffs.
He pointed in all directions and raised his brows.
Ahnee knew his meaning and then thought,
'Why do not the Gods fly below the clouds?'

'Yet, who am I to question the Gods
To guess their meaning, needs or wants?'
Then she pointed between North and East,
Then widened her arms from East to West.
She bent to the ground and made a mark,
Then made the sign for day and dark.
Seven fingers are seven days to be walking.
Nimrod with his people would be talking.
Did the Gods wish to journey and when?

Cornelia Benavidez

Ahnee bowed her head, put hand to heart.
Then she pointed back to the people's caves.
Nimrod nodded, smiled, as she walked away.
Ahnee told her parents what the God wanted,
They were surprised by this announcement.
Puzzled yet, still they readied for come what may
For the directions given that were a long way

Long ago, the people brought themselves to settle here.
It was more pleasant with more game to share.
They realized ten days' further lay the other's road.
They found that this area had been battled before,
The people wished only peace, not war.
So, they had traveled on another ten full days
To come upon their beloved caves.
Here, with planning and work, they were fed and safe.

Yet, now with six men by her side,
Ahnee led Nimrod and his brother nigh.
Each time they stopped to rest they learned signs
To better understand each other and pass the time.
The days came and went quickly, and they arrived
By tall red cliffs and a deep river side.
Setta now showed a passage that they followed.
In single file, they walked in this wonder.

The high walls opened to a large space.
From there were other canyons to pace.
'Here!' Setta cried, 'We shall build new homes!
That this will be a new place to call our own.
Here is where we must build and thrive,
For we must do more than just survive.'
Ahnee saw Setta's satisfaction
As she was troubled with a question.

She lightly touched upon Nimrod's arm
And knelt to draw upon the ground,
For her people ages long knew this land,
This place of beauty, wind, cliff and sand.
The spirits of this place had hidden dangers.
Without man fire here had no food or fodder,
Its river path curve had carved and wandered,
The hidden dangers here came by water.

The people of the skies had great wisdom.
Soon work commenced and all were kinsmen.
A city emerged, from stone and cliff was rend,
Dwellings, temple and channels for water.
The base was laid for a great tower.
It seemed every day there was a new wonder.
Few were those left in the caves all alone.
Ahnee loved to learn but missed her home.

As the city grew so did its great art,
For Nimrod it was the growth of his heart.
Marriage and children with humans was forbidden.
Nimrod loved Ahnee yet kept it well hidden.
But the power of love knows no walls,
Whether Gods or men, they follow its call.
Under the stars and by secret hand rite
Nimrod and Ahnee became husband and wife.

Ahnee's mind was quick and clear,
The new knowledge she did not fear.
She embraced all the new mysterious ways,
Still, deep in her heart, her Gods she did save.
The old, with a few families, had stayed behind.
Her parents came to see the city and the mines.
'Our beloved daughter of the lovely long hair,
Remember our love and your home in our care.'

Cornelia Benavidez

From the great ship came works of great magic,
The wonders so great beyond faith and logic.
Ahnee soothed the people's concern and fear:
'Did not these wonders build and heal?
Did not the Gods supply every wish and need,
The clothes we now wear, our children they feed?
The Gods came down to the earth and chose them,
What others can say the very Gods know them?'

And time moved on and yet stood still,
Work was hard, yet the people were fulfilled.
In the places of the Gods, plans were made,
Setta lead the talks of who would go or stay.
'It will take more time for our ship to be repaired.
This small planet is both so rich and fair,
These people here are as our own children,
We will teach and further shape them.'

Nephilim
Part III

Take heed, my sons and daughters,
May we not become blind or falter,
As in the ways of Gods and men.
Let us not stumble by fear and sin.
Let us pray for wisdom and grace,
For like them, life we must face.
Take heed of the tale I must say,
Perhaps to find ourselves and they.

The land above and around Ahnee teemed with life,
The river had fish with forest and fields ripe.
Nimrod became a mighty hunter
Of resource, fat game and every monster.
It was in this venture an idea bloomed and grew,
Nimrod knew what he must do.
To his brother Setta and council he presented:
Why another community must be settled.

Cornelia Benavidez

It worried Ahnee to leave her people behind,
Yet this she must do for the sake of their coming child.
Nimrod said, 'We must make ourselves indispensable.
What we have done is, for Setta, incomprehensible.
He still does not know how many are we
That have found friend and love to fill our need.'
'He is a God; how can he not know?' Ahnee questioned.
'He is focused and busy in other directions.'

So, Nimrod was clever as well as strong.
He had thought ahead so Setta saw no wrong.
Ahnee is needed for she has the expertise,
For near here is our mothership for all you need.
'I will create a colony of resources and food,
You will receive fresh every full and new moon.
By having the hunting fields far from this city,
With what you maintain here leaves you with plenty.'

Now Ahnee and Nimrod made great haste,
There was not a moment to linger or waste,
For all would soon know what they have done.
It was a comfort to Ahnee not to be the only one,
Even the Goddess Saula had a husband and child.
The child was hidden with her husband's kind.
The sister Goddess hoped for a change in the tide,
Yet, Nimrod knew they were only buying time.

Hard they worked. The die was cast
For as long as they could make it last.
With tools and in a small ship flew Ahnee,
With dreams and hopes to be free.
Yet the people sorrowed for her loss.
Was this a sacrifice and the cost?
Their Priestess and Princess was spirited away
From family and friends who had no say.

They moved far into a land of giant trees,
Thick and tall as far as the eye could see.
With no cliffs, they dug into a hillside,
Carved into the stone and made the pit wide.
Nimrod honored the land by building a temple
To please Ahnee and the Gods of her people.
For Ahnee it was such a tender sweet gift
For her husband, the God, to think of this.

The Gods worked swiftly under forest canopy,
Houses must partly under the ground be.
For if other Gods flew by or might visit,
Children could be hidden, and nothing be amiss.
Nimrod spoke to Ahnee of the birth of their child,
What must be done to keep both her and child alive.
'My sister will give you medicine and peace
Then we will open your belly while you sleep.'

Those words sounded frightening, yet Ahnee was calm,
Was she not tended by the love of these Gods?
The time came quickly, not a day too soon,
For Ahnee could barely walk or move.
The hands of Saula moved sure and swift,
Soon the hands of Nimrod held the precious gift.
Ahnee woke with the sun as the day was breaking,
Nimrod said, 'Beloved, here is the child of our making.'

'She has greeted the sun and been bathed in water,
Take her to thy breast, Ahnana, your daughter,
For *gift of wonder* means her name
Much like her mother, though not the same.'
Ahnee clasped her child in her arms,
Kissed her face and was only slightly alarmed,
For child's skin shone golden, with eyes of blue light
And a head full of hair bright shining white.
Ahnee cradled the child to her breast,

Cornelia Benavidez

She pondered if she would pass this test;
To be a good mother both kind and wise,
For her child who was half Divine.
Nimrod gave her a gentle kiss
'My lovely Ahnee, now I can tell you this:
Though in giving birth you must endure pain
The blood of the Gods is already in your veins.'

The shock on her face was clear and plain.
'My Lord and love, please explain!'
Nimrod sighed and held her hand,
'How much do you know of the tale of man?'
'Our sacred chants say our spirits go to the stars,
But our bodies return to the earth's heart.'
'Yes,' he answered, 'In its way your wisdom is true,
Yet, there is more to this story than you knew.'

'In your years I am ancient, I am young in mine.
When your story started it was before my time.
Why you call us Gods is partly our long existence,
Also, our great knowledge from stars far distant.
To feed our machines and ourselves we must fly
Across the universe of space, so radiant sublime--
Truly the playground of the Gods.
These are the worlds I am a part of.'

'Long before your time my people found
A blue green jewel by its sound,
For every kind of life has its song or chorus.
In the heart of darkness this wonder called us.
Yet, we too, have our faith, ways, and rules,
Perhaps our surprise made us fools.
Though this is what I should never confess
For here was found growing soul consciousness.'

'This world was so full of the magic of life
Of so many types and so many kinds.
A world of resources! A world of play!
Of course, there were those who wanted to stay.
Yet imagine our shock and annoyance
When we discovered a people among all this,
Very simple and shy and different.
This now forced a change to our intent.'

'This very world is your guardian and God.'
'Yes, I know.' Gently did Ahnee nod.
'My people sought our sacred laws to bend,
And not leave this earth alone to fend.
After all, with just a little knowledge and help,
The people could do more for themselves
And we could have what we want and need,
All in the guise of a good deed.'

'So, by our knowledge, craft and art
We set ourselves high and apart.
The Gods among you we became
To rise in song and prayer to fame.
You trusted us with body and soul.
Some of us saw you as an empty mold
To be shaped and then refined,
Like a kind of animal yet still a kind of child.'

'Your people came to work in our mines,
You lived and worked for both truth and lies.
To marvel at the great buildings, we fashioned,
The more we taught you, the more you questioned.
Changes we made inside you to made you smarter,
More pleasing to our eyes, stronger and faster.
Follow our words, that is all that matters,
Explore and harvest, over this earth we scattered.'

Cornelia Benavidez

'We had lost our center and fallen from grace,
There were those of us that this could not face.
Some took a sky ship far past your sun
To tell our people what had been done.
And they came upon us like fiery Gods
To destroy our work of what they could find,
For we will not murder our own kind.
Nothing further would be done to mankind.'

'Yet, for our people, punishment they must face
For their blasphemous fall from grace.
Stripped were they of ships, tools and home,
Separated over earth far wide and alone.
A few did run, one or two escaped,
To live with nothing would seal their fate.
Those who were young and could be forgiven
Left with our people back to the heavens.'

Ahnee's face now ran with hot tears,
'Nimrod, my love, why are you here?'
'We only came to observe,
When our ship crashed to the earth.
There are our tools to make repairs,
Important parts and fuels had not been spared
So, all of these we must find,
The rest takes work and much time.'

'Setta knows our mother ship may never fly,
And we may never be found here is why.
Yes, we explore looking for what we need,
But never should we have come here!
This world is to remain to us unbidden,
To visit this world is long forbidden.
Yet this was the story of our grandfathers,
We wished to just see these hidden wonders'

'Setta is no fool and knows why
We have gone far away to hide.
But what he must not ever know,
It is possible for children to be born.
If our people come to rescue us,
I wish Setta to be innocent
And then we can only pray
That they will allow me to stay.'

'And also, Ahnee, more you must know,
This child of ours will much faster grow.
We must also think and plan our way,
For the day will come when we cannot stay.'
Saula came then, bearing bandages and gifts.
She agreed with Nimrod it would come to this.
'Ahnee heals well no bleeding or swelling,
Let us be thankful for this great blessing.'

The babe had snuggled at Ahnee's chest.
They both looked with love at the child at rest.
Yet now Ahnee's heart filled with fear,
Her eyes spilled over with many tears.
Nimrod gently lifted his child and wife
And cradled them to his side.
'This I say, pray and vow,
That we will have peace someway, somehow.'

Nephilim
Part IV

Weeks, months and a few precious years flew by.
The people prospered, Setta bid Nimrod to come nigh,
For all the people he was their mighty hunter,
All wished to see him and do him honor.
Saula would stay and watch the children
Since they could not be brought with them.
Ahnee was happy to soon see her mother and father,
She knew that much would be expected of her.

Ahnana was already the size of a child eight-years-old.
Nimrod said that soon her growth would slow.
From Saula, she was already interested in healing.
Ahnana was a child of quick wit and deep feelings.
The child's beauty and intelligence was astounding.
For Ahnee and Nimrod their fears were silently mounting.
They gathered the outpost to discuss where to go hide.
After plans were made, then they said their goodbyes.

It was with many thoughts and mixed feelings
To come back to the city and what were they seeing?
There from its midst stood a great tall tower,
Setta had wasted no time to show his power.
They stepped from their craft with a few friends and guards,
Dressed somewhat formal to show their regard.
Ahnee smiled and waved, though her heart was aflutter,
Soon she was wrapped in the arms of her mother and father.

For Nimrod, the greeting from his brother was warm.
He placed aside the worry from what was forewarned,
And his brother's countenance was as bright as the sun.
In such a short time so much work he had done.
The city wound from ground to high in cliffsides,
The people had prospered standing tall and fine.
The very air was filled with joy and anticipation
All looking forward to this time of celebration.

Ahnee, by her people, was swept away,
While Setta bid Nimrod to talk and stay.
Setta wished to show Nimrod his own palace cave,
The growing city, and the tower he made.
Nimrod had once seen the tower's broad base.
He was amazed at how quickly the tower was raised.
As they slowly mounted its long stairs,
Setta explained his reasons and his plans.

'Surely by now your people must know,
Nimrod, I wish for you to come and stay home.
Your people shall continue your work to provide
Meat and goods for both our sides.
Saula I know there has made her way,
Your pilot can fly goods and she can stay.
You are beloved, even Ahnee, by all of us,
We wish the return of their princess priestess.'

Nimrod drew in a deep breath and climbed on,
Taking a precious few seconds to sort his thoughts,
'Brother, though I may miss seeing you every day,
Hunting is the passion that gives meaning to my ways.'
Setta stayed silent till they reached the last stair,
'What of your love of Ahnee? You think I am not aware?
Her people know in their own quiet way
What other reason would she so long stay?'

Nimrod and Setta now walked to the tower's wall
To look over the view and the great fall.
So long he had thought about such a day,
What he could do, and what he would say.
Yet, it was Setta who broke the silence.
'Nimrod, as a child you were both brave and defiant.
Certainly, if we never go home to our world
We will make new laws as the future unfurls.'

'Yet, still now, Nimrod, you must listen to me.
For the sake of our people for the love of Ahnee'
And Nimrod's face was calm as stone;
'What if, my brother I wish not to go home?'
Setta's face now all his emotion hid,
'I do not think this is a wish you can win.
To have a consort can be forgiven, even understood,
But to desert your family, your people never would.'

'You know the laws, Nimrod, that which we call sin,
The complications and difficulties therein.
I also guess there are others with love such as yours.
There must not be more, or chaos ensues.
We have the love of these people as we are like Gods,
If they lose this faith what becomes of us?
If we are found soon by our years,
There must be only joy not any fears.'

Nimrod spoke sharp, 'What is it that I do not know?
I have reason to believe that we are not alone.
Have we had a sign from the stars?'
Setta turned, 'No, it did not come from so far,
I have come to believe on the other side of this world,
They are other star travelers, or some of our own.'
Nimrod stood still and thought desperately,
That so quickly he must protect his family.

Ahnee was welcomed home to a ritual bath after her flight.
The ways of the Gods and people combined that night.
Ahnee asked for her mother and for privacy.
Disappointed, the women left for what they must not see.
Ahnee's mother came from a long line of midwives.
She gasped when Ahnee showed her the thin line.
'I have never seen a cut heal on a body so fine,
My beloved Ahnee did you have a child?'

'Mother, what I tell you hold close to your heart,
No one must ever know what we have spoken of.
You have a grandchild. Her name is Ahnana.
She is part of the Gods, for Nimrod is her father.
I do not know why having such a child is forbidden,
She is born from love yet must be kept well hidden.
I cannot say what the Gods and fate will allow,
The sin is long done, she is a girl already now.'

'The healing ways of the Gods have kept us strong,
Even though our caves are like a world far gone.'
'Ahnee, we all have missed you, our people sigh.
Your father fears that our ways will soon die.
Of course, we will long to see your child,
Yet, you may be safer living in the wilds.
I do not know what can be done,
Could Setta forgive a child of one?'

Ahnee closed her eyes. Her head was sore.
She dare not say that there was more.
She was given then a dress, fit for a queen,
This was a little strange, she was far from serene.
Escorted from her mother's by the Gods' guard,
Ahnee hoped nothing with Nimrod and Setta was marred.
She was surprised to see before her a small ship.
She then was told gently to go into it.

Nimrod was dressed in gold armor with sword.
Everyone greeted and treated him as a great Lord.
He walked through a sea of smiling faces.
He gracefully nodded while his heart was breaking.
Yet his eyes were soon bright alighted,
When he saw Ahnee with his brother on the dais.
Nimrod raised his great arms and deep bowed low,
Setta therein placed a golden quiver and bow.

The people then gave a great cheer.
This filled Ahnee's eyes with tears.
For how long this joy could last,
When the people would know what has past?
Nimrod stood so Godlike, handsome and tall,
Was this the coming of their star-crossed fall?
They feasted and played four nights and days,
Yet, both longed to see their beloved babe.

At this time, Setta told Nimrod 'it now does matter,
For me to know how you will answer.'
Nimrod asked for respite, a few days to think over
All the changes to be made and in what order.
He and Ahnee met the best they could secretly,
When would they go and the best time to flee?
Still, Nimrod was with Setta when guards ran in,
'Come quickly, my Lords! A great starship!'

Centered over the tower, a bright shining disk.
Nimrod said to himself, *now it comes to this.*
Setta stood frozen, Nimrod asked for his bow.
'Come, my brother, let us quickly go!'
They flew to the tower, to the landing part way.
Then prepared themselves to walk the rest of the way.
They walked in silence till at the top they stood,
The tower in shadow, as from a great moon.

Yet what greeted Nimrod, to his great surprise,
Ahnee was brought to stand by his side.
Setta stepped a-ways away and then he nodded,
Running toward them came Nimrod's daughter.
She was swooped up in her mother's arms,
Yet, Nimrod was strangely calm.
'Ahnana, has Saula come to harm?'
'No father, she ran after, she fought the guard.
She begs forgiveness for she knew I was safe.'
Nimrod and Setta's eyes met, filled with pain.
They must have been watching for some time.
Setta spoke, 'Some of your people escaped their sight.
Those they will capture to be scattered far and wide.
I told them you were seduced by a woman's wiles.
I begged for this moment, it's such little time,
So, that at least you could say good-bye.
Nimrod, you must give up this sinful romance,
This is our last hope and your last chance.'

'We are your children!' Ahnee cried to up above.
'We are only smaller yet my husband I love.
You say you will not harm or murder your own,
Yet you break our hearts and leave us alone.'
Ahnee's brave words fell on deaf ears.
Only a beam of light answered her tears,
Holding Ahnana close to her breast,
As Nimrod bent to place a kiss on her lips.

Then, like a King he strode into the light,
And like a God he began to take flight.
As slowly he rose, he pulled out an arrow,
And cocked it in his great golden bow.
With a mighty pull and a great cry
He let his golden arrow fly
Straight up into the giant ship
When it was released from his grip.

Cornelia Benavidez

Nimrod fell as the beam of light disappeared.
He was not hurt as Ahnee feared.
Ananna cried out and ran to her father,
Then fled to the small ship to join his brother.
All sped away, the small ship now well-loaded.
Like a volcano the tower behind them exploded.
Setta cried, 'what you have wrought on us!'
The city was in fire, smoke and chaos.

'I have tried so hard to forgive and understand
That the people are not animal but also man.
Now it is out of our say and our hands.
It may go so far as to destroy all the lands.
There is no going back now,' Setta said bitterly,
'We will be here forever and never can leave.
What shall we do and where will we now go?'
Ahnee said softly, 'we cannot go back but we can go home.'

Nephilim
Part V

With Additional History

The Gods destroyed the great city as the people fled.
Those the Gods captured scattered far over sea and land.
Some were taken, but Nimrod they could not find.
It was not long until they left all the earth behind,
And survivors of the city were already telling the story
Of how Nimrod defied the Gods, and how he was worthy
To be a true king, with Ahnee as queen to lead them,
As the people explored the new meaning of freedom.

Ahnee and Nimrod became rulers crowned,
Built great cities under the ground,
For fear the Gods would return to hunt them down.
From there their story was told and begun.
Ahnee's mother and father returned to their caves
To carry on their faith and sacred ways.
They must this keep safe. They did not doubt this.
They taught the children wisdom and justice.

Saula came to visit with her son and lover,
They soon returned to the people who had helped her.
She told that those captured were taken or sent far away,
Around the earth they had been placed.
There, they would be watched at a distance.
She said that there had been no resistance.
'Setta had the only small ship
Which he now has kept very well hid.'

Over the long years Setta told tales and rumors
Of the power of women who brought men to ruin,
And because of their sin, they begat monsters.
And the pride of Nimod was the sin he fostered.
And in the guise of their beauteous child,
Was said the curse of childbirth and nature so wild.
Ahnee was now turned the deceiving whore,
Turning from her makers, ever wanting more.

Yet we the people, I say, know your worth and truth.
You carry the seeds of Nimrod from the day of your birth.
Over all the earth know that you have blood relatives,
Scattered was the God seed of those called Nephilim.
Though many of the people's ways have been twisted with lies,
We hold the truth within us until all will come to realize
That love, truth and life lasts for all time.
We are the flowers of stardust, born divine.

The Points of the Story That Were Most Important to the Young Man's Family

It was stressed to me that Nimrod came from the stars, yet I suppose it could also be thought possible that Nimrod and his people came to earth by some sort of interdimensional ship. It was said that Nimrod had a brother, in some cultures they say a twin, but in the young man's oral family stories he was an older brother. That the Nephilim were Gods compared to us, and that these Gods had been visiting humankind for a very long time, was clear. It was also conveyed that in some ways they considered us their children, or in some cases we considered them spiritual parents, for they changed and influenced us in many ways for various reasons, including to evolve faster, which some among their kind or associates did not think was a good idea.

There was a strong faction of these beings that felt we should just be left alone and in the peace of innocence. There were others who did not agree with this, for various reasons, and they violated the agreement, either by accident or intent. Once this was done, some chose to stay on our earth to defend those they loved, or perhaps they hoped to uplift humanity on principle. Again, others felt that no good would come out of this in the long run, because already humanity had been given mixed messages and values that would cause inevitable conflict. Also, what now complicated matters more was that some of the Gods had mated with humans. This was considered an unfair advantage at the least, and an abomination at worst, and was dealt with by scattering the offenders around the earth, so the knowledge and potential progeny be more spread out. As further punishment, they were left with minimal tools or technology and any places built with such were ruined.

The young man's family felt that Nimrod not only stood up for his family, but also for all mankind on principle. He felt that we had a right to be free to evolve as we wished, but that we also should be entitled to our history and have the right to grow into the ways of the universe. Also, that though there was a brief golden age, the truth of what happened became lost. We have forgotten that Nimrod was like Hercules; a hero of the people. That to be free to live and grow as we will, we must be heroes ourselves. That all people are unique and should be valued no matter what our bloodlines are, or of what blood and DNA mix we may be.

It is our right to know who we are and what we can become. In the long run, maybe we have something to teach even the Gods, because of who we are.

All I have ever known about Nimrod, until this work, was what this young man told me, and that Nimrod was mentioned in the Bible as a mighty hunter, the founder of cities and a king. It was not until many years after first hearing this story, that I heard or saw other tales of Nimrod from other sources.

In Arabic literature, Nimrod founded towns. It was said that he saw in the sky a black cloth and a crown. He had one made for himself and was the first king to wear a true crown. All crowns came down from him. Older traditions say he ruled in Syria. Later works, that were accepted by Christians, say he ruled in Sumer and that he was an arrogant, evil tyrant, who was the builder of the tower of Babel.

In some Jewish lore, Nimrod left Shinar and moved north with his twin sons, who were also mighty hunters. They settled in the mountains near Kurdistan. There are many legends in Armenia and Hungary of the giant Nimrod and his twin sons. Yet, it is also said that Nimrod started fire worship and was an ancestor of Zoroaster. I have heard whispers that Nimrod's daughter became a Goddess who founded cities and that, through her family, much knowledge was passed to humankind such as astronomy, astrology, medicine, mathematics, and the arts.

In some Jewish works, Nimrod becomes connected to Noah and to Noah's sons. According to the young man that I knew, it was in his oral tradition that the true story of Nimrod and his family could be found, and all other cultures have only small fragments of the truth. This fragmented knowledge is scattered all about the Middle East, Eastern Europe, and beyond. The young man also suggested to me that the mocking and genocidal persecution of oral traditions, and their accompanying arts, levelled at all tribal people about the earth, was not just about conquering land grabs, but an attempt to eliminate all other timelines and facts of human history.

It is for these reasons, that the fight for freedom is not just about being conquered physically, but about the freedom to know, to speak, to create and grow in peace. It is to hold precious those things, ideas and people who inspire and uplift us; encouraging us to aspire to be whole in both body and soul. For it is then that we are refined and ennobled in every way and become worthy to be child of the universal heavens.

Poems of Doorways Toward Awareness

There are poems that are more like a conversation with ourselves that we let others into. Then we have word paintings. These word paintings are lingual art, which are necessary so that we can portray an experience, a thought of profound implication, or intellectual eureka, as accurately as possible and share it with the outside world.

Poetry becomes more than telling a simple story, or beating out a verbal rhyme, or even an expression of some type of ecstatic high (though this too can be valid). They are the profound moments of insight, emotional awakening and spiritual vision that are very difficult to convey. Poetry is more than up to this challenge.

So, when the Muse graces you, there is a connection made; a lightning path of perception. Whether this comes through joy, sadness, or in contemplative otherworldly awareness, it is here, through the medium of poetry, that the poet can lead others through their feelings and the intellectual processes of their own mind. In these gifted moments the poet, and the force that flows through all artists, allows everyone to glimpse what shamans, poets, mystics, philosophers and others have always seen or deeply felt.

Cornelia Benavidez

Threshold

The mythical puzzle
　　The mystical cup
　　　　The banquet of life
　　　　　　I must sup.

The labyrinthine doorway
　　The sacred sacrifice
　　　　The dance at the threshold
　　　　　　I must survive.

The Stag

The path on the headlands rose steadily up,
The air was full of salt and sagebrush.
The ocean waves sang ever more softly,
As they climbed higher toward the sun.
The stony path was oddly full of life;
Song birds hopped, sang and scattered.
Shrews, voles and chipmunks
Scurried alongside the path.
Wind twisted cypress and pine.
They were three, so young and bright,
Laughing with saucy tongues;
The two boys and the girl.
They walked ever upward,
Speaking of magical things.
The starry-eyed young magi,

Cornelia Benavidez

The wary doubter,
The romantic witchling,
All full of fool's innocence
And innocence's bravado.
They now reached the top
Of the rocky coastal rise,
Surrounded by rocks and shrub,
The ocean far below.
A sudden silence wrapped itself around them.
'Why is it now so quiet?' asked the girl,
'Hush!' called out the magi boy
'Something is about to happen.'
The doubter chuckled as his lip curled,
'Can't you just enjoy nature for what it is?'
'Look!' called out the girl with joy.
A falcon rose silent in the air before them,
Flew over their heads, diving behind a rocky rise.
Three heads followed the bird
And now stood with mouths agape,
For there, behind them stood a great stag.
His many tines reached out like fingers
Ready to capture moon or sun.
Yet, it was the falcon who once again rose
To hover, wings spread, between the great horns,
Before flying over their heads once more.
The noble stag snorted and walked away,
Slowly, with great dignity, down a small stony trail.
'It is a sign, it is a sign,' whispered the one,
'I can't believe what I just saw' said the other.
The girl ran to the rise and climbed a rock;
The hillside opened before her below.
The boys scampered down the path to look.
All that greeted them was wind in the trees
And the return of the singing birds.
The great stag was nowhere to be seen.

You Asked

You asked
What do you see?
With eyes open or closed?
Sighed I
Both, you said
With a nervous smile.

With closed eyes
I see waves of emotions
The vibrations of a teeming sea
I reach into it and sometimes
It reaches into me
It is diaphanous book
Whose pages I read
A flickering movie
Shadow dancing their scene
I see tender dark mysteries
Like a burlesque tease
Of what can be revealed
Of what might come to be
And I am filled with inner questions
But have no mouth to ask
Beloved, can you tell me
Is God's heart bigger than all this?

With open eyes
I see longing and judgment
In every eye including mine
I struggle to shield myself
From the ravages of time
I see a world that wants to be... more
Like all the wisdoms I have read

Cornelia Benavidez

A celebration of every song-filled vision
With pride in the smallest stead
My open eyes drink in the wonder
Of color, shape, smell, and touch
With a love so deep
It can hurt too much
Yet all the horrors
They too are there to see
I recoil at the thought that
They too might fascinate me

Then the loathsome, soothing voices
That coo... nothing really matters
There is nothing
You can change or do
Only time can heal that is true
But time can be like a lover
That never sticks around
It fills you
With insidious distractions
Then it lets you down.
Yet, from somewhere I remember
There is a divine design
God's love must be
Greater than mine.

You asked
What do you feel?
With eyes open or closed
Ask I?
Both, you say
A bit of worry in your eyes.

With closed eyes
I have felt a young man hiding
From the soldier's rifle

And the desire to end life
Like a venomous knifing
He cursed his pounding heart
And the water in his bowels
The taste of terror in his tears
And the dryness in his mouth
I have felt...
The soul that longs to be a child
Like butterfly wings beat and
Plead be mine... be mine.
I feel life justified
In every creation
Then see the vomit of our betrayal
We call human nature
Now, in the poet's hand
I have felt renewal
When in the preacher's voice
I have felt refusal
Yet somehow I have to believe
That the Gods' love does feel
Even more then these

With open eyes
I feel thankful just to be alive
To feel the sun, the wind and even
The tears from my own eyes.
I feel I demand too much
And then again not enough
Afraid I will lose my spirit
If I get too tough
I long for perfection...
Redemption from every fear
I need to be alone
I need to feel you near
I feel I ought to free you
Set you free from all my need

Cornelia Benavidez

Cut through the barbed wire emotions
That have so long imprisoned me,
And I pray that every hope-filled blessing
Will grace this earth sometime
And yes, that Divine love
Will prove stronger than mine

She Walks

She walks a razor's edge
The fine line that sets the middle road
She is dressed in woven moonbeams
Her sacred totems travel with her
Mirroring her light, following her light.

Her light defines the razor's edge
Between bright and dark
Between touch and thought
Between the sublime and the heinous
Her whisper breathes out, choose.

She emerged from the space between the stars
Created and embodied both Moon and Sun
She formed both valley and mountain
Her fire holy blood red within the earth
Her tears the waters of life and death

She walks down the mountain
Singing the song of desire and love
The razor's line splits the ground
There it widens unto a golden road
That all may walk and dance upon.

She stands at the razor edge
A silver sea, a luminous purpled sky
Our lady of peace and righteous wrath
Awaiting our choice
Awaiting our love

Poems of Sorrow, Anger and Rage

Victor Anderson once said to me that sorrow, anger and rage are double-edged swords of emotions. On one side, they are the potential weapon of unbridled destruction, on the other, a fine edged tool of justice leading toward healing. He told me more than once that:

'Anger and sorrow can be the forge for some fine damn poetry.'

Here he would laugh and add; 'and a holy rage can align one with the Gods, but only if there is not a pathology underneath its cause, for then, so often it will end up in tragedy or a big fine mess at the very least.'

Sorrow in poetry can range in tone from worry and concern, to the outcry, in written form, of deep loss and pain. Our human condition is displayed in symbols expressing the intimacy of the loss of love or overwhelming murderous rage. Yet, in poetry we not only express the moments and wounds of our life, but we find the keys to have the chance to express and explor our harsher emotions. Here we can find the hidden doorways of resolve, acceptance, wisdom, healing and ultimate transcendence, despite our pain. So, we may gain solace as well as rise above and gain control of the sorrows, anger and rage that life may invoke in us.

Blue

I asked someone to tell me blue
Its science, its feel, its hue
So many words lost
In so many thoughts of you.

Blue heavens
Endless wells
In blue seas
Captured fire.

My tears fall on dry ground
Filled with blue and no sound
So many words lost
In so many thoughts.

Blue with thunder
Like a comet I fell
Now empty words
The dark yawning hell.

Blue the smoke
Between our worlds
Can hope now be trusted
And courage be unfurled?

Peace, the color of healing blue
Spirit kissed with elemental truths
Let me be submerged then too
Let me be reborn in you.

Cornelia Benavidez

In the Moment

Three times thirty
Ten times six
Minutes, hours and years to mix
What do you treasure?
What do you own?
The skin you are in?
Your honor or phone?
Words that sing
Be it in love or wisdom
Will not matter if you do not listen.

I punish myself for expressed emotion
For loss of dignity in the commotion
I punish myself
For a missed perception
I punish myself
For each imperfection
I punish myself
For what I cannot control
I punish myself
For feeling alone

Three times thirty
Ten times six
Around I go to pick up sticks
What have I gained?
What have I lost?
Was there a reason for the cost
Of my pride, my time and love
And the purpose so long sought?
The sun beams down its good intention
The searing burns are rarely mentioned.

Days

I remember the days
When my heart had no room for suspicion.
I remember the days
When, in the eyes of another, I could not fathom malice.
I remember the days
When my smile would light the world, causing
Fear, sarcasm, and doubt to shatter and scatter
Like so many nervous mice.
I remember the days
Before my spirit became so bruised that
My soul fell into a stormy sea,
I became a lost treasure,
Now, it's you I see so much like me.

We both remember days.

Cornelia Benavidez

The Dance

She looks up at him
His heart sinks
In guilt and resentful strife
She loves him
He can't imagine why
That same old story
That is so much the same
A hardened heart
Misplaced love
Cowardice conquers shame
Is it not interesting
How one can run from truth
Hidden in the beginnings
Of an indolent youth?
He hates himself for being afraid
Has a few drinks to play it safe
He found himself in a job
He was not really proud of
Still, could not help that inner shine
So, this is what she came to find
Blind sweetness to walk in his land mine
She calls him friend, sees all his wishes
The spiritual doubts, the longing musician
He gives her an ear, she lends him a hand
Thoughtfully listens to his fears and plans
She the careworn flower blooms anew in
The guise of his smile and smart cynical views
Such trust must have a higher purpose
She opens her heart to let out her secrets
The loving and sharing in all her sweetness
Afraid yet still daring
To believe it could be true

That she had found someone to love
Who could need and love her too
But this dear little flower how could you know
Most people will despise what makes them grow?
From all mirrors they will run
This is why you now are no more fun
And then comes the painful silences
No more smiles or midnight confidences
She wonders why the averted eyes
The half-hidden sneers and out and out lies
Scornful of her tearful questions
Accuses her of manipulations
Hurt-filled righteous anger on him bore
He shrugs his shoulders, heads for the door
I am not cruel only honest
You are not what I really wanted
The sad little flower now should accept this lot
That all that was shared is now forgot
And yet though often this may be true
He will learn Karma will stick it to you
He will be looking back at his regrets
And the sweet little flower he will miss.

Cornelia Benavidez

Bonds

Together or apart
Thinking of all of us
That have run out of words
When all our tools fail us.

Not knowing how to forgive
Anger shut, fearing to live.
We become grateful when
Someone else sings our heart.

May this sing out to you
Who may feel lost or alone,
Not knowing what gives
Not knowing what can be said.

Please consider that I may not know
How I have fallen short,
Or I may be mistaken
In feeling so wronged.

Yet, waiting here with me,
Even after this long while,
Are the memories of our time,
A garden of words with my smile.

For Ariel

From around the world springs Ariel:
Your name, the spirit and power of air
Yet also the wielder of fire.
I mourn you and bless you.
Close my eyes to see you
With that bright smile
And those sad eyes.
And I can still feel your arms about me.
Your spirit whispers in the wind,
Both in sorrow and new wisdom.
Light your way, light your way,
Let us all find one another
Under the great world tree,
Between the worlds,
By the great silver sea.
We shall tell great tales and sing,
And God will be alive,
And magic will be afoot,
And your spirit will drum again,
One day... One day.

Cornelia Benavidez

For Farrah and Michael

Her limbs graced the printed page,
Giving curves where there are none.
Her smile beamed, an innocent Cheshire cat,
Our all-American girl in wonderland,
While his body grew, and morphed before our eyes,
The young prince that dared to be King,
In a gilded wonderland and Picasso world gone wild.
They were our stars, a kind of sister and brother,
To become fallen soldiers in the battlefields of art.

Questions

Did I fail you?
In my quest for a moment's peace
A moment's rest
A few moments of distraction.

Did I fail you?
Every time I believed you
Still held your hand
Fought for you in so many ways.

Did I fail you?
In my quest for once to be true to myself
To my wishes and my desires
As you so easily do.

Did I fail you?
In my honest confusion
That you twisted
To suit and justify your anger.

Did you fail me?
Or perhaps yourself
When you swallowed what was fed you
A lie easily sweetened by indulgence.

Such a bitter taste,
Such a sad fate.
When words failed us,
The silence screamed.

Cornelia Benavidez

For Old Friends and Lovers

I wish that I could find a way
To let us smile and find amends.
I wish that I could find the way
So, you know I hope
You are with friends.
I wish that we could find a way
To trust our spirits once again.

I wish we would find a way.
I wish we would find the way.
Click my heels three times.
I wish we would find a way.

Over the river and through the woods,
Down the White Rabbit hole, we fell,
Hand in hand, Alice and Red Riding Hood,
Through thunderstorms and big bad wolves,
Smaller, taller in the mirror house,
White knight and Cheshire cat.
Can we escape the looking glass?

I wish that we will find a way.
I wish that we will find the way.
Click my heels three times.
I wish that we will find a way

Thin Line

Making money by a thin line
And playing righteous passion
With a snarl and angry eyes

Making money on a thin line
Taking on the man
With screams and clever lies

Making money on a thin line
Looking so rebel hot
And yet so unaware

Making money on pain and confusion
Making money on rage to use you
Making money to look damn good
Making money you play the fool

Making money on a thin line
No one can tell wrong from right
Reaping the fear and sorrow of the blind

Making money on a thin line
A faded faint boundary
With no wrongs or right

Making money on that thin line
We sell our souls before our time
What kind of world will we leave behind?

Cornelia Benavidez

Another Perspective

The loneliness of your friendship
Sits in silent waiting
Caresses my emotions
With its taunting tempting.

The loneliness of your friendship
Hides in all your charms
It bedevils my spirit
It beguiles me to harm.

The loneliness of your friendship
As you ignore my pain
You justify so wisely
It is your greatest shame.

I am Not the Windmill

I have been assailed and paled
I have been poked by a lightning mage
Of his guilt, self-pity and universal rage
Clawed by winds of mood you wage.

I am not the windmill

I have been left in the eye of the storm
The cold hail leaves me bruised and alone
I beg the rain to wash away my sorrow
That I might be free and warm tomorrow.

I am not the windmill

When will you be free of that old horse
That dark, rusty chain-mail
And that sword of stone?
Walk away from your screams and moans.

I am not the Windmill
I am not the Windmill

Cornelia Benavidez

You Can Only Try

I told her my dream.
She laughed,
Thought it was some scheme
To get her down
From the high that she found.

Lost for more words,
No answer came clear.
Tears betrayed my fear.
The dull cold eyes softened.

Don't cry for me.
I'm just fine: look at me.
I'm flying high, no worries have I.
The world can just pass on by.

I walked her home that night,
Watched her wave a happy good-bye.
It's OK, I need to be alone tonight.
So sweet was her smile.

Such a lonely feel to my room, I sigh.
I awoke at light to the tears I cried,
I guess you can only try
For that night she died.

The Scream

Why is it only when I scream
That I feel you somewhere, deep inside?
Why is it only when I scream
And I have no place to hide?
Can you hear my cry?
Can you feel my aching sighs?

Billions ask where can you be?
Their bleeding hearts, an endless sea.
Billions ask, why can't you hear
That life itself is what we must fear?
On the wind do I hear your sighs.
Is this rain the tears from your eyes?

Why is it only when I scream
So deep for you?
Straight from my soul
I want to know
I need to know
Will I ever know?

For Sarah

I knew you were kind
But I did not know how
To get to know you.
I knew that you were
Smart, talented and
Very determined, still
I did not know how
To fully get to know you.
The river of life carried us
Far and away while
Memory grew boggy,
Till the news came
That you had slipped
Gracefully into the lands
Of love and light.
I wonder if somehow
I could have known you better?
And like to think perhaps,
Somewhere in sometime,
We will meet again.

Cornelia Benavidez

The Lie

You lie.
Enrobed in silks and satins
And shining tempered steels
And guarantee of revelation
When dying time sweeps near
No need for roll call
You know we have it made
When just a few buttons
Can end the whole damn race
How long have we waited in line?

You lie
The drunken masses
Expecting none divine
While reveling in torture
Blind saving the blind
No need for roll call
No heaven if no goals
Only all the pleasures
Of power with no soul
How long have you been waiting in line?

You die
Like the beef you slaughter
And barely wondering why
Without the grace of a star reporter
To tell us the time
No need for roll call
No left or right in space
No matter who you see
It will be the same face.
How long have you waited in line?

Poems of Philosophical Romance and Life's Musings

What a gift it is to just wonder. To lie in the grass and gaze upon a blue sky filled with racing clouds. As a child, to run to your mother and father to ask: 'Why is the sky blue?' Then to be told the stories of the gods, goddesses, helpful spirits and animal creatures. Those who painted, long ago, the first sky and brought to us the power of the sun. To both hear and read the stories of our human heroes, legendary and historical, from so many ages and from all over our earth, fills one with curiosity and hope.

The fact that so many themes, poems and complete stories have survived thousands of years to continue being passed on, even further down the ages, speaks to their importance to the human spirit. It is from these quests of curiosity that courage and desire are born. Here, hidden in the ancient ages are the secrets of universal magic, the science of endless time and ever-changing creation. This great cosmic Goddess gave birth to us with all our endless possibility. She holds our secrets, yet dares give us wisdom, and the gift of the savor and flavours of love. Our tales and word rites can tease or nudge us to dare to reach for spiritual guidance and for the right and the means to reach to other realities.

There are answers everywhere, I was once told, by my Grandfather, with a wink, though truth is often hard to find. It is our life's work to awaken and to engage in what is truthful, meaningful and right.

Bargain

Today the air is full of rain and the promise of thunder.
The coyotes howl in frustration,
For food sustains yet does not fatten,
So, we bargain and the forest nods.
This year the trees cling to green,
As I cling to hope and memory.
The words of the old sage whisper,
Did I not say that the space between the stars
Is far from empty and alone?
Did I not say that I would escape
The ravens and the crows?
Did I not dance in clouds and lightening?
Listen now.
Take comfort and joy in the fruit of the land,
In the hands that weave and knead both cloth and bread,
Dread not the cold nor the icy breath,
For yet still the Gods give their gifts
While man seeks passion in life and death.

Victor's Day

Today is such a bright and life-filled day;
The sky so blue and filled with cherry petals,
Dancing on the wind like Japanese fairies.
I miss you so, but somehow cannot be sorrowful.
You are a part of the words on the page,
A part of the warmth of every candle,
The sound of the waves and the roar of thunder.
You were Her cauldron as you sang Her nature.
It is sweet with love,
Sharp with power.
Her song prevails,
Your life prevails,
Borne on His great blue wings
And Her endless light.

Cornelia Benavidez

Thinking of You Almost Haiku

The Beauty of your voice
Echoes in my mind
A distant drum vibrating.

The Beauty of your words
Beats in my Heart
An inner clock singing.

The Beauty of your spirit
Speaks in many tongues
While your Blackheart listens.

The Park

The park speaks to me after midnight,
For only then it can be heard.
It whispers in lamp-lit shadows,
Hums through the fog-kissed dirt.
The trees are witness to my murmured prayers:
The poplars applaud my humbled heart.
Inside the great cypress lie Fairy realms
I wish to be worthy of.
There is wisdom in this darkness,
It beckons at every turn.
I seek it as a thirsty traveler,
The glare of day has left its burn,
The moon crosses my face with silver.
For a short time, I too am night.
The park speaks to me and I answer
To every star upon the sky.
The wind sings and weaves sonnets in my hair:
Kiss me.
And you might hear the willow's song placed there.

Cornelia Benavidez

Spring Wakes

There lies the stillness of a mighty work,
A vibration stirs and comes to life,
Its whisper the song of the God's wife.
Roots reach out like twisting hands,
Seeking water, food from the motherland,
While tender rising shoots stretch for light.
Oh, so fragile, yet what great might
From humble worm to the birds that soar,
Each blade of grass and babe is born.
Sing songs of joy the Goddess has awoke!
On the earth, man plants both fruit and grain,
While singing songs of love again.
Now the birth of butterflies and moths,
Deer and bear, fox and boar.
Sweet maids dance, the flowers in their hair.
Bold young men bare-chested ride the mare.
Our time of thankfulness, love and hope,
Within the rich soil of the earth.

Elemental Flame

I am falling through the sun
Wings of flame spread around me
I speed through space, breathing with fire
I am dreaming of a blue pearl
Hope blooms as I fly like a phoenix
In the darkness, she is garbed in blue and white
The heat blends my flames to a pure red aura
And I am born

Cornelia Benavidez

Their Spirits Shine Like Rainbows

Is it not a wonder, my brothers and sisters?
That flowers smell so sweet
That the scents of tree, bush and vine
Will adorn our altars and grace our hair,
The smells as varied as colors or music in the air.

Is not a wonder my brothers and sisters?
That from dying bloom, a bud appears
That grows forth to plump ripeness.
Again, a new scent, a new color invites
Tastes that thrill the tongue with desire.

And is it not also a wonder all my children?
In leaves the colors of the rainbow,
In dying they find your eager hands,
A last joy before the awaiting arms of earth,
There to sleep sweet until Spring's birth.

Yes, is it not a wonder to all people?
That the grain and gourd rise to fullness
To be food and thatch, bowl and rattle.
Look into the darkness my friends,
For their spirits shine like rainbows.

Four Sons of a Mother

Who wishes to go a-seeking berries?
Asked the kind young man.
Three boys' heads turned,
Fast as owl heads.
Jumping up as one,
'Where shall we go?' they cried.
Happy hands gathered pails,
Running feet over meadows sailed,
To forest and field this Lammas tide.
As the sun made for its rest,
Triumphant boys returned well spent.
We picked blackberries and late cherries!
Mouths, hands and faces warrior-painted,
There is so much and more to come!
We will take a bunch home to Mom!
Oh, the blessings of Lughnasadh,
Corn and grain the fruits of love,
Ripe and full in warm air you hovered,
Then plucked and joyous gathered,
By these four sons of the Mother.
A blessing for the table.
A blessing on the woods and field.
A blessing on their household.
A blessing I have seen.

Cornelia Benavidez

When You Know

That moment of awareness
The sucked in breath
The white light flashes
Thought like a lash
That settles to a deeper hue
Knowledge paints a darker blue

Evil

Evil has been spreading itself once again,
That oozing swamp of fear and arrogance,
Its warm mud falsely inviting to despairing souls,
Gaseous bright lights lure the unwitting,
To its many death filled holes.
This swamp revels in itself.
It only knows the hunger it has,
This kind of evil spreads itself, beware,
Through those that even think they care.
It moves so swiftly, oozes so quietly,
Most do not know it is there.

I have stood at its edges; it mocks me,
As it mocks you and everything.
It hungers though it's fed every hour.
It hungers for what is rightfully ours.
It is gleeful for our madness.
It grows fat with our sadness,
Ravenous for our pain and fear.
It longs for every broken scream.
One drop at a time it licks our tears.
Evil's children are a spreading weed.
Open your eyes, you can see it feed.

Ironic then, our cup is filled
Of all of nature that man has killed.
Yet, in the midst of this darkness,
Even when it lurks within its lair,
We tremble and cry to be spared.
So evil now torments us easily,
Even by our own hand,
Setting child to child, women to man.

Cornelia Benavidez

By greed this feeding frenzy begins,
It slimes with shame and ignorance,
It's the rattling saber, the grin of the reaper.

Brothers and sisters, we grow weary
Of this danger, filth and stench,
Still, listen to this secret,
Evil yet can lose itself.
Today may be its feast day,
And yesterday its banquet,
Our love within can always wake us.
Have we not come for a mother's kiss?
Or the hand of a beloved so long missed?
Somewhere, someone longs for us.
A child, a dog, a garden needing our touch.

The endless words wishing to be sung,
Let not bitterness freeze your tongue.
Yes, the swamp hungers for all of you,
For life itself so beautiful,
The Divine dance is full of grace,
Let not your choices be full of waste.
More violent and cruel evil does become,
Sensing our rising consciousness.
We can win this battle if we never forget this,
Though the whole world it seeks to dismember,
Ever we will return until this we remember:

The power and love of the eternal Divine is within us.

Pele

Went to visit Pele at her volcano home
Climbed to her very edge
And knew I was not alone

She wrapped round me like a lover
And as I felt her oh so near
She then whispered in my ear

Smell the stream with my sulfur rising?
And taste it in your mouth?
The earth is a body and I am its blood.

Mount Shasta showing her volcano roots

Cornelia Benavidez

Moon

You are watching
We are watching
Circle to circle
Face to face

You are watching
Us come to light
By tiny dancing steps
Blind but hand in hand

We are watching
Your beauty and promise
Sacred thy mysteries
Reposed in lover's arms

Dreams of Agape
Our White Lady of Love
Our Lady of Reflection
Our Lady of Madness

We are watching

Remembered

We were horses,
You and I,
From the days of your nervous youth
And my tossed mane bravado.
Introverted, you nibbled at the stall,
While I cantered in larger corrals,
Sometimes breaking for far fields.
They came with soft words and ropes,
Told me I deserved the silver bridle.
The saddle fit so well.
I do not think I went quietly,
Though I do remember when
They say you kicked the padlock,
Bolted through the door.
And then I awoke
To remember
What it meant to be the horse once more.

Cornelia Benavidez

May Day

They come, strong shining lads
They come, carrying the ribbon tree
They come, the laughing maids
They come, bearing flowers for the tree
They gather round
Plump wives with children
Young lovers holding hands
Grandfathers bearing fiddles
Grandmothers holding babes
Warriors of earth bear kegs of ale
They cheer the planted tree
Ribbons wind waved
Caught by eager hands.
They will dance the song of spring
They will weave the course of the stars
Greeting friend to friend, heart to heart
Today we turn the tree, calls out the bard
We plant the seed in the name of love
This is the tree of all beginnings
The tree of wishes and of dreamings
This is the tree of Hope
This is the tree of Joy
Here is where the world turns
Here the moon chases the sun
Here is where we become one.
The music swells, feet dance the beat
To weave a spell
And steal a kiss
Up and under
So, and so
Round and round and then
Let go

The Golden Box

There is a golden box that sits pristine
On an oaken table high in a turreted tower.
The tower's windows rise tall to arches
To frame the roaming green hills
That race to far off mountains
Against an ever-changing sky.
I climb the narrow winding stair
To find the heavy oak and iron door.
Moved, it protests against my presence,
As it opens to the austere room,
Yet it be filled with a luminous light,
For Sun dances on the windowsill.
A beam reflects upon a box.
Soft, I walk to gaze down upon it,
As my hands curl about its coolness.
I know it is heavy, yet it can be carried
To be placed on the wide windowsill.
Here we both will be warmed by the sun,
As I sit upon a tall backed chair
And with gentle hands unlock.
There inside is another, smaller golden box
As all these mysteries tend to be.
This too I place upon the sill.
There the music box may freely shine golden,
And I may have my fill with its unfolding.
I admire, as if anew, all its intricacies,
Tenderly lift its lid to long lost melodies.
Though all be peace so beautiful,
It is here that I close my eyes
So my ears might linger on each note
Before chased away from the ones behind.
Now I take the larger box, replace it on the table

And spy a mirror on a wall catching the light.
I shake my head and give a gentle laugh.
No more to be fearful of mirror's sight,
I tip-toe to its judgment,
To find beauty's eyes and hair still abundant.
Breathe deep and then sigh reassured,
I now return to my golden treasure,
And inside its deep red velvet folds
Lies a wealth beyond all measure,
It is here inside safe from all harm,
A pile of tiny golden charms,
Each perfect and so life like.
I take them out one by one,
They sparkle bright in the sun,
And each has its own melody
And each has its own story.
The Golden box can play them all,
Or if I wish it, it be will be silent,
As I ponder upon each glory.
There be babes and children there.
In perfection, each is made,
Maids and men so handsome
It could make your heart break.
There too are wise, wizened grandmas,
With aged yet noble old men
An almost endless host of creatures
That look so sweet, alive and fine.
Symbols and objects,
Curios of all kinds.
The sun now slides to afternoon.
The windowsill was well-filled.
Unrushed I refill my box.
Yet, before I close its lid,
I reach between my breasts,
There, safe in a little pouch,
I find a tiny golden owl feather.

This too I place inside my box,
For here in this tiny feather
Is a perfection of what we knew.
Here it is safe from the world's corruptions,
Even safe from me and you.
These moments of sweetness,
Laughter, trust and love,
Innocence and courage
And accomplishments attained,
Each charm of my memories
Never shall be chained.
It is the golden treasure
I visit again and again and yes,
There will come that time when I arrive,
And the mirror that never lies tells me
I must take my gold and away must I fly.
Then, in the course of gods and men,
And in between the stars,
Where we heal our wounded hearts
And find the love that cures,
I will share with you my treasure
And you might show me yours.

Poems to and for Divine Presence

The fiercest passions and longings that arise in the human heart are all related to love, desire and spiritual or religious devotion, in one degree or another. The love of God or gods, the love of the quest to understand our own soul and purpose. The hope and faith in a divine plan and Universal Spirit that not only gives life but gives meaning there too. This is where poetry soars and snatches our attention away from mundane everyday life, compelling us to consider more.

Whether poetry is telling a sacred story, teasing us to humor, expressing our human longing for worthiness and admittance to what is hidden from us, be it in word, accompanied by music, performance or art of any kind, we feel the call and return again and again to it. Storytelling and poetry, with their accompanying arts, become an invitation and path to something bigger then ourselves, as well as to realities beyond our kin or imagining. Such constitutes a rallying cry for unconditional love and truth, the outcry of ecstasy in the giving or receiving of it. This passion and emotional enlightenment is the spiritual consciousness that is so desired and sought after, that it can be worth the price of death. As we endlessly seek to share and describe and relive this quest through the eyes, words and feelings of all beings, it awakens us to the possibility that this gift, this truth, is there ultimately for all of us to find.

The gateway to knowledge, wisdom and love is the door that we all may knock upon, and it will be opened to us. It is the word and song calling us towards freedom.

Mother Mary

The embodiment of serenity, acceptance, kindness and love,
My whole childhood I would seek you out,
In grottos, backyards, cemeteries and churches.
There I could slip in and gaze on your face.
I would behold your sacred child
and rejoice at your mysteries.
Mother of forgiveness,
Mother of healing,
Mother of power,
Mother of miracles,
Mother of mothers,
So gently you smile and extend your hands,
Biding us to love and wisdom.

Hope and Star Dust

It was not so long ago,
When we were truly young,
Full of hope and sweetness,
Valiant battles to be won.
The magic of those voices
We joined in song and call,
Praying for the better world
That would embrace us all.
The notes dance and ripple endless
Through hearts, space and time,
And, though some fear to believe it,
It is still here and there for all to find.

This was a painting I did, at around eighteen, from a picture that was taken in the German or Swiss Alps. My parents always kept it with them.

Cornelia Benavidez

Jesus, Hero of the Innocents

Jesus, Lord of the heart of your people,
Your sacrifice an offering of grand design,
Or are we still blind to the depth of such crime?
The old and babes in the arms of women
With men embrace their children and brothers
Came to walk your words about the earth.

It was in the play of innocent children,
Their sweet laughter in your ears,
That you dreamed a time of peace and freedom.
Out of the endless years of wars and pain,
This was your vision, most holy child,
To become the man to hold us through.

So, we can believe in our healing
And the wisdom in your words.
May we find in us your courage.
May we somehow find your will
To not turn away from those who suffer,
In all the human ways we are afraid to face.

Your love shines through the ages,
To lead us through darkness,
To reveal what is not right
To redeem that which is twisted,
In your love's cleansing light.
May we reach to be refined.

Lady of Stars

Starry Maiden, Starry Fair,
White and Gold shines through your hair.
I beheld your sacred child,
Playing, laughing, singing wild.

Starry Maiden, Starry Bright,
Came to me all dressed in white.
You whispered secrets in my mind,
I dreamt of you a mother kind.

Starry Lady, Starry Shine,
Your hand casts the measure of time.
You showed the ageless earth,
The endless love in your mirth.

Starry Lady, Starry Light,
Your silver sea calls all to death and life.
Your terrible beauty freezes and enfold.
Your loving embrace then makes us whole.

Starry Women in moonlit night,
Holy Mother, Crone and child,
We walk upon your golden road,
At your crossroads lead us home.

Cornelia Benavidez

Season of the Sun

It is the season of the sun,
Of ripe berries on tree and vine,
The season of the field,
The works of women and man.

In the season of the sun,
The waters run for life and play,
As children search out thy mysteries,
And young lovers seek the shade.

It is the season of the sun,
Let us be joyous and cautious,
Let us value our time,
In this season of the Sun.

Moon Rite

The Moon rises proud and golden
A comforting mystery
Our Lady of many guises

The Moon turns opal
A peeking flirtatious wonder
Our Lady in the trees

The Moon sets, a gentle silver
A shrouded bidding inspiration
Our Lady in the sacred waters

Blessed are we with her cycles
Blessed are we in her gentle light
Thrice blessed are we in her might

Cornelia Benavidez

When Spring Meets Summer

When spring meets summer,
The Lord and Lady hold hands,
The day is long and in perfect balance.
I set my altar with red and yellow roses
And a bowl of apricots and cherries,
As if dipped in sun and blood,
Their colors light up the room,
Their scent gentle, sensuous with promise.

Persephone dances for her mother,
The God readies his chariot,
The fruit is the rising and setting sun.
I place a perfect fresh, fat, white egg
With the fruit and flowers there.
I then muse and sing to myself,
Father Moon, Mother Sun,
Father Sun, Mother moon.

I have a vision of leaping flames,
A warm wind is cast
With the rising of great fiery wings.
With a triumphant cry, it rises
The great phoenix of lava and flame,
Circles the sun and disappears,
As the moon rises golden
The sacred child of a new day.

The Voices Are Ancient
A Hallows Call

Listen and heed!
It is the time of being still
The time to open thy heart
To the feelings of all loss.

Listen and heed!
For it is the time of all ancestors
Their voices as ancient as time
And as close as the last goodbye.

Listen and heed!
For the doorways that open to us
Now let us call across the great divide
Give of our spirit and receive blessing.

Listen and see!
It is the light in the lament
The magic of the woodland Fae
And their voices are ancient.

Blessed

I found Jesus
As a little child.
An Angel whispered
'Love is your guide.'

I found the Buddha
In the heart of the tree,
Showing the way
To an inner me.

I found the Gods of India
In my traveling dreams,
A palace of nagas
Color-filled themes.

I found the Lord
In a forest deep,
As the Goddess woke
From Her long sleep.

I found the drum
And the magic flute,
Australia to Africa
In all its Native roots.

I found the song
And I hear the word,
Around the world
On the wind it turns.

Margaret on Lammas

I remember you the most in August,
Though your birthday was in July.
I still smile at your Pele lava hair,
The sunflowers that would grace your Altar,
While your fingers and hands would express,
Through art and crafts, to typewriter or piano keys,
The wit in those sharp cat green eyes.
Lammas is its own special wisdom
When you open your heart, you would say,
Yes, it is first harvest, and it foretells the fall.
Pay attention to the comings and goings in life,
They are the chapters of your story.
Bloom like a sunflower, be full of seeds to feed others.
Be joyful in life to burst like the dandelion.
From yellow-gold to white, then let the wind
Carry your song for others to find.

Cornelia Benavidez

Epoch

In the dawning of knowledge, before there was none,
And man had no powers only his Gods,
Were these Gods merciful and kind
To have kept knowledge from our eyes?
In the dawning of knowledge,
When men and women were sung,
Fear and joy was given from above,
The people worshiped and loved.
Would knowledge their peace overcome?

In the sunset of magic and the dawning of Satan,
Men now cursed and swore the Gods were tainted,
With the desires of our flesh
And the whims of our ego.
On the river of time where will this flow?
We are now in your image.
Is this not what you wanted?
Now you cast yourself into mystical voids,
Far from the mockery you started.

In the dawning of science and the rise of power,
You claim our souls and hearts to follow.
The rise of evolution and its price to borrow.
The right to kill from an ivory tower,
In the sunset of innocence till the dawning of tomorrow.
Did they leave us forever to our own devised sorrows?
And did they curse us, all of humankind,
As we ourselves flee to the skies
Knowing deep inside that it is to find them.

Poetry as Shared Invocation, Worship and Prayer

Writing poetry is most often thought of as a singular process. The exploration of one's heart, mind and soul brought forth in words. This is a very private affair, of which we are fortunate to be voyeurs, when the words are not our own. Yet, there is room in this deep well of inks to make space for a partnering in this inner psychology and spiritual intimacy. This happens in the creating of poetry when writing rites for celebration and or worship. Happy memories come back to me in working or speaking with Margaret or Victor about writing for holidays or for a working such as a healing, marriage or other rites of life. For a time, I had a student – Timothy – who I enjoyed writing with. We wrote together 'Brigid Invocation' and he inspired me with 'Elements' and 'Poet's Mind'

This shared work, be it in the writing, or the voicing aloud of written work, can take several forms; most commonly from the lyrical set to music or to the dramatic stage play, which can arc from the comical to an epic historical story. In its romantic form, poetry speaks for, or of, the beloved, be it in the classic uplifted courtly love, or to the shared words of a lover's passion. In the world of faith, creating together provides a taste of the act of creation itself.

Poetry, in all its forms, is an offering of shared, written insight and intimacy. There are many examples of shared creative works, whether to be spoken aloud, or acted out for an audience, as an inspiration or educative piece. Yet, it is in the creation of the sacred rite, be it in temple or circle, that offers us solace, hope and connection with each other and the realms of nature and spirit.

In our modern times, there are so many styles that are the wells and cauldrons of our wordsmithing. We express our faith, hopes and longing in spiritual odes, rites, hymns and rants. Poetry that evocates and invocates has a profound effect on both our mind and heart. When we recite these words that have formed in our mind, to come out of our bodies in worship and rite, on the breath of our speaking, something very special happens for us. The very air now trembles with intent. We sense the eyes of spirit upon us and our hearts open to interaction with the forces of the divine world, and with that which we hold and cherish with a love most mysterious and dear. It is in this sharing and bonding, and even in the letting go, that humans can explore all the mysteries, from the bittersweet, to embracing wisdom with soaring rightful pride. It is also through poetry that we speak with the divine forces that wish to express themselves in our world.

In the broader scope of such philosophical things, it may not really matter whether this inspiration comes from an astral muse or from our higher self, our own emotional inner joys and turmoil, or the Great Spirit of God, however we see him or her. What matters is that when poetry has been birthed forth, therein lies great power and possibility. As soon as another's eyes or ears experience it, they too are moved.

Poet's Mind

The mind of the poet
Has eyes that are forever
Roaming inner horizons
Exploring philosophical riddles
Seeing deeply and wondering why
Pleading with the Divine
Calling dreams into form
Spinning endless word shapes
Within the fluid landscapes of life
From the depths of the inner mind
As a poet and lover of the muse
Weaving the word paths of inspiration
From the darkness into light
Searching for gold found within
The reality of our star seed birth
We laugh and cry while connecting
Threads that hold us together
Knowing tears and testing truths
Insisting upon the holiest love
Only the angels once knew

Cornelia Benavidez

Circle Opening

I call upon those of our ancestors
Let us join hand and hand within this sacred ring

Hear our voices that echo through space and time
Your attention and love, a divine offering to us

Awaken within us our fire to learn wisdom,
Awaken our passion that we may know truth
Open our clearest path to peace and refinement
Which is in the work of the Divine on our hearts.

Brigid Invocation

To thee, Mother of the Flame,
I offer up my prayers to thee Brigid.
Sacred Mother of the Hearth,
Your presence comes forth
Like a bright flaming arrow,
Breaking the soil open that was left bare
From our long cold winter months.
Bright one, shining one,
Rekindle the light without and within us,
Inspire us to create by hammer and hand.
May our words be touched by your fire.
Let our art become holy by thy flame,
Our hearts be filled the warmth of hope.
Then, like the birds of the air, we too shall sing
As the earth begins its return to new life.

May Day Blessing

Golden is the sun
Golden is honey
Golden is the heart of amber
Golden is the fire
Golden is the bee and
Golden are the flowers
Golden be the mead upon thy lips
Golden be that fiery kiss
Golden is a bright May Day
May all good things light your way

A Prayer and Rite for Spring

This is our rite of spring,
To be thankful for every flower that blooms
And the fruits thereof,
To rejoice at the birth of both lambs and wolves,
To know that each cycle of stars that marks our time is a gift.
Yes, today let us look within, into the winter of our heart.
Open our eyes to what worked and did not.
Take the seeds of wisdom
And plant them in our minds to grow.
Pray for truth, pray for love,
Pray for this healing to rain upon us.
May we find our way to walk a better road,
So that all may drink thus,
Knowing we are blessed.

Cornelia Benavidez

In the Light of Day

Listen oldest ones.
Harken young ones.
Hear us as we pray for love, hope
And for compassion for all life,
For laughter to return to those whose
Hearts and spirits have been beaten,
Held down, twisted by greed and evil.
We pray for the healing and protection of the earth
And for all her sacred waters, salted or sweet.
May we all return to the ways of light.
May all our hands work for peace.
Where there is hate, let there be love.
Where there is fear, let there be hope.
We pray for all to open both hearts and minds,
To value the precious gift of time,
To seek compassionate logic and understanding.
May we rise to our place in the realm that is sacred.
May our eyes reflect this light,
May our ears listen for the sacred songs,
May our hearts feel the living rhythms,
May our fingers work with joy,
May our feet ever walk in beauty,
May we remember the grace in all life.

Autumn Equinox Invocation and Blessing

We call and greet you, our Lady and Lord.
We give you thanks for these first fruits of harvest.
We give thanks for the balance of night and day.
Bless these offerings this autumn equinox.
May they nurture us
As we work and play in your great wheel of life.

Cornelia Benavidez

Goddess of Hallows

Ahhhhh, Mother Earth,
You cover yourself,
With a quilt of wild color.
Your children of earth frolic
Before the great sleep.

Ahhhhh, Our Beloved Lady,
Wrapped in your cloak of stars.
Your bright moon shines
Down on the last harvests.
Sustain us through winter's cold breath.

Hail to Mother of Life.
Hail to the Lady Ruler of Death.
Hail to the Child of Promise,
Turning to a New Year.

The Elements

Earth

Gnomes sitting upon mushrooms,
Waiting deep within the forests.
Crystals and fossils, the old bones of the earth.
The scent of trees, flowers, and soil
Fills the nose, grounding us to the land.
By the warmth of the day and
In the stillness of midnight,
We call to thee,
By Persephone, Demeter, Gaia
Cernunnos and Pan.
Let us be blessed as we walk
Upon earth's sacred ground.

Air

Sylphs floating like feathers,
Through the air at dawn.
Winds that blow both soft and strong
Over the hills and across the plains.
Our minds touched, awakened
By each breath we take,
By each word we sing,
By Aradia, Urania, Thoth,
Hermes and Mercury
We call thee, air.
Know we are blessed
By thought and breath.

Cornelia Benavidez

Fire

Salamanders frolicking in flames,
Bright fire, your light illuminates
From the sun's ring of flame
And the flow in the earth's red veins,
To the tending of each hearth.
In renewal, the phoenix flies,
Passion rises by blood and desire.
Sacred pure flame we call to thee,
By Brigit, Pele, and Agni,
Vulcan and Prometheus.
We are blessed when you ignite
In your warmth and in your light.

Water

Undines play through rivers and falls,
Fluid and flowing, crumbling walls,
Guides to the wells of intuition.
Water sustaining all life,
Be thee of rain, brook or ocean,
Quench or cleanse all of us,
Who desire to be filled by lusts.
We call to thee, water
By Yemaja, Mari and by Aphrodite,
Neptune and Osiris mighty.
We are by thy spirit blest,
Let us drink to our body and spirit.

Spirit

That of the unseen hand,
Born from space's dark womb,
Dancing between stars,
Flowing from thought to form,
A part in the heart of all things,
The dreamtime of all souls,
The song that sings to all worlds.
By our Lady and our Lord,
We call for what is true and divine.
Open our ears, open our eyes,
Bless us with your current,
And in your grace, we are reborn.

Cornelia Benavidez

The Winter King
(A Yuletide Tale)

The King went a-hunting on a day cool and green,
For a flash of white had caught the King's gleam.
He rode proud and bold into forest dark forbidding.
His horse snorted with caution yet kept its footing.
Heart leaping with hunt lust, the King spurred his steed.
A white sow would soon grace his table feast!

He rode strong and hard from flashing white to white.
How could so large a sow be so fast and light?
Then there it stood and with what great art,
For in his path stood a gleaming white hart.
He raised his spear let out a joyous cry,
'Hart or sow thou shall be mine!'

The spear found home in yonder tree.
The hart disappeared in twinkling speed.
The King once more took upon the chase,
Deeper in the mossy woods did he race,
Till his frothy horse did raise high on his hoofs.
The King tumbled to the feet of a great white wolf.

No horse, no spear, yet the King held no fear,
For the wolf turned toward a large bear cave.
Snow now fell on this King so brave.
He struggled to rise then lay to rest.
A white owl called his name as he slept.
Gentle hands laid garlands on his breast.

Lo, what did this King behold in divine sleep?
The treasures of ages that make men weep.
A golden summered land of peace.

A shining silvered endless sea.
A blinding flash of purist white.
A star-dressed Goddess graced his sight.

'Come, be my lover, brother and child,
Thy people's king but as priest be mine.'
'How can this be I must be born anew?'
'So, shall you be, in my world and in yours.'
Her arms so tender around him held.
Fear, doubt, lust, all angry shadows fled.

There in her arms now came a sweet cry.
She kissed the babe and he became a child.
The child in turn grew to run and dance;
She waved her hand and he became a man.
Now she kissed his lips and each eye.
He awoke to bird song and a horse's neigh.

The branches of pine that made his bed
Now flower-covered scent filled his head.
Soft he rose to a new sacred quest,
To make a vow upon the hallowed land,
To never forget this Goddess gift:
Now a Man, King and Priest the forest left.

Margaret and Victor

This work would not be complete without a few more words about my mentors and friends, Margaret Korwin (also lovingly known as Dama) and Victor H. Anderson.

They shared a fierce devotion, both to nature and the written word. They released their poetry as one might free caged birds. Victor's wife, Cora, patiently saved money to print '*Thorns of the Blood Rose*' and later, '*Lilith's Garden.*' Margaret did the same with '*The North Wind's Daughter*' and '*Petroglyphs.*'

Both Margaret and Victor were highly intelligent, generous, talented and loving people. They were full of humorous mischief, righteous indignation, and at times, impossibly stubborn. Yet, to sit with them long enough to fully understand the length and scope of their knowledge and experience, was a privilege and, at times, a wonder to behold. Both were musicians, although not everyone knew this. Both were fond of children, science, cats, and a good book. Both were well-versed in history, mythology and the lore of many traditions. Margaret and Victor, furthermore, were gifted with wit, insight, intuition, and an insatiable curiosity, all exercised with their spiritual gifts and large loving hearts. They taught me to trust myself. They showed me what I already was, as well as where I might go.

In the 1970s and 1980s, the New Age movement and the New Pagans were falling over each other in a race to discover and uncover old traditions or create new ones. As the High Priestess and Grandmaster of their paths, Margaret and Victor reinforced the deep love of nature with which I was raised, while they were teaching in-depth the ways of tribes, religions and cultures around the world.

This became a tapestry I could look upon while following my personal thread through this tight, bright weave.

I combined their many teachings with my childhood faith and experiences, as well as with what my mother taught me about finding peace within myself through connection with the divine, either in silence or through the arts, both being doorways. These three also taught me that life is a journey and that all steps in a journey, even the stumbles and falls, are valid and are counterbalanced with humor, healing and understanding that leads to growth.

Everything that one learns, or treasures, is never truly left behind. You carry it with you. It has its place in your heart, for such is love in all its forms.

The next two poems I dedicate to Victor and Cora Anderson, with the last poem, that follows, to Lady Margaret who inspired it.

Cornelia Benavidez

The Beginning

Photo by Henry Buchy

The Great Goddess sighed,
For lo the space was vast,
It was herself and yet not herself.
Timeless the eons dance about her.
I wish to know myself in all my parts,
She mused – and dreamed of shape.
In space she imagined boundary and form.
Therein she carved a great black mirror
And beheld herself reflected,
In all her great terrible power and beauty.
She felt within herself endless possibilities
And, for the first time, the pangs of loneliness.
Her loneliness grew forth to a great desire;

The pangs of birth came upon her swiftly,
With joy, wonder and unimaginable force,
A sundering and rendering birth shone forth.
She cast out her embodied reflection,
A great God brighter than a thousand suns.
My Son! My Beloved! And Myself she reached,
As he reached out unto her with great love.
My Mother! My Sister, and Myself he saw.
They embraced and intoned the first sound
And their love was a great making, an ecstasy
That became the first word, that became the first song.
From this union shone forth the first stars,
Yea, from the loins of the Star Goddess and her Lord,
Who draws forth her light and paints the universe,
Came forth the beginning of all things.

Cornelia Benavidez

The Lord of the Painted Fan

The Lord spoke and said to the people:

I am the fiery bright shooting star.
My power crackles in the north and south,
In walls of light and frozen ice.
I am the lord of many names.
I am the great bird of flame
That paints the heavens you've come to know.

None can hide from my ecstasy,
For I am everywhere in the earth and sky,
As I move weather, the thunder my cry
In green, indigo purple and blue hues,
Even in depths of the earth I choose
In mineral, stone and crystal I move.

I am hidden in the veil of space
The darkness cannot hide nor contain me
In time, in mind nor in the depths of the sea.
I am the root, the tree and the leaf,
Shaped and moved by the hand of man,
I stand tall and I expand.

For I am the Lord of the painted fan.

Cornelia Benavidez

Trinity Invocation
Calling of the Holy People

You who are
> Maiden of the hearth,
> Mistress of the cauldron of our bellies,
> Mother
>> Stirring the dream stew
>>> Of your tears of joy,
>>> Your tears of pain,
>>> Your tears of ecstasy
>>> Your tears of profound peace.

Share with us
So that we may know your name.

You who are
> Lord of the tower
> Master of the book of attainments,
> Father
>> Building the dream
>>> With your cry of passion
>>> Your cry of sorrow
>>> Your cry of desire,
>>> Your cry of profound knowledge

Share with us
So that we may know your name.

You who are
> Child of the dream,
> Spirit of the key to all imagination
> Sacred Child
>> Living the dreamtime
>>> Our of time of wonder,

Of our time of loneliness,
Of our time of blame,
Of our time of love.
Share with us
So that we may know your name

You who are
Great Mother, Father, Child,
Movers of all Nature,
Dreamers of the seen and unseen
Help us to forget our lies
Our lies of fear,
Our lies of power,
Our lies of weakness,
Our lies of separateness.
Share with us
Illuminate the paths of truth,
So that we may know our names
And not be ashamed.

A Very Basic History of Poetry

In the Beginning

Poetry, and its sister arts, have been with us in one form or another from the beginning of spoken language. One can only wonder which was first sung and written: perhaps the cry of a child for its mother, or a cry to the skies for rain or a plentiful hunt. Then again, it was our first, great primordial cries to the gods of nature that drove humankind to share and keep records of its achievements and insights through chants, poetry, song and art. Those chanting songs beat to the heart of the tribe, their words evolving into the bloodlines that memorialize ancestral deeds, as well as one's relationship to the whole. They speak and sing of the danger averted by the brave, the satisfaction of full bellies, or the birth of a healthy child. These 'event' songs, coupled with the changes of season, inspired celebrations, during which human beings would watch one another dance the beat of their joys and successes. Another living memory would consequently be generated in tribal song and create history. It must have been then that a young lover danced for his beloved and thereby discovered the courage to say:
  'I want you. You are wondrous to me above all others.'

The epic and enduring fireside tale needed a form to burn into memory, so that details were not so easily changed. This is how chants with rhythmic spoken words came to be, with rhyme soon to follow. So, the groundwork was laid for the telling of humankind's oldest, most enduring and controversial professions; first in the tales of the Hunter/Warrior, then those of the Healer/Shaman, Lover/Artist and the Visionary/Poet. It is this last one who would chronicle, throughout the ages, the deeds of daring, as well as his or her own conquests of the heart and of intellect, all with soaring metaphysical perceptions. The words so generated would grow in detail and creative form; a timeline to connect us back to our beginnings. This would invoke in us the waking of our muse, our very soul, to our deepest romantic and spiritual needs, as well as our most ancient rages and battle cries. This is poetry as it was, still is and forevermore will be; our souls' written lifelines throughout our ages.

Though varied, the facts of poetry's written history are fairly easy to find. Looking back to ancient civilizations, long before modern paper, we find its first treasures on stone, clay, copper and papyrus, and later on cloth and rice paper. The Epic of Gilgamesh, from the 4th millennium BC, was set out on clay tablets that were found in what is now Iraq. The Gilgamesh tale is based on the exploits of an historical king. Likewise, some of the oldest known love poems were found in Sumer/Mesopotamia, and also on ancient Egyptian walls. In 2004, National Geographic magazine reported on newly-translated holographic writings, most likely older than between 1539-1075 BC. Those poems and songs are about love and romance in ancient Egypt. Moreover, the subject matter and techniques used are very much the same as in any culture or time. The following is a short, lovely example of what has been found and translated:

The Flower Song (Excerpt)
To hear your voice is pomegranate wine to me:
I draw life from hearing it.
Could I see you with every glance
It would be better for me
Than to eat or to drink.
(Translated by M.V. Fox)

Cornelia Benavidez

In the Jewish psalms that comprise parts of Christianity's Old Testament, we also find poems and hymns of both love-struck eroticism and deep spiritual devotion. The Greek epics, such as *The Iliad* and *The Odyssey*, gave us enduring heroes. In India, the great Sanskrit epics, the *Ramayana* and the *Mahabharata*, still cast their magic spell over the ears and hearts of humankind. As far as we are now aware, the *Mahabharata* and the Tibetan epic tale of King Gesar are the longest epic poems preserved in writing. Such epics tell of gods and goddesses, the creation of the world and humankind, great battles between good and evil and the sweeping passions of both gods and men.

Furthermore, deep in the bush and jungle, on far-flung islands and mountain highlands, epic stories and transcendental inspirations are told mouth to mouth and song to song. Some of these poetic expressions are so sacred they can be only whispered, while others take shape in dance, carvings and art of all kinds, ranging from the decorative to the utilitarian. Epic tales have survived to uphold the culture of native people and to move the minds of modern men and women to rethink one's place in the known universe, as well as in the great beyond. Within these written and oral threads, poets of all cultures and religious persuasion find solace and are assured of the necessity of their craft.

It would seem that the call to interpret and express what is most profoundly felt, from our deep desire to connect with what seems unreachable or unknowable, is a primal human need. Be it from without or within us, the drive to relate these inner feelings and perceptions is more than a history or one's deep inner shadows, but often what we learn when the Muse calls us to the wellspring of the Goddess herself. The Divine Female, whether Mother Mary, Kwan Yin, Mari or Bridgit, is our spiritual mother whose language is poetry. It is how we best speak to Her and She to us. Her Divine Consort embraces the magic of these words and thus tempers His great force. And through poetry's balance of love and passion, creation and destruction, we live. On this divine breath we create and grow.

Such is the history and mystery of poetry and its power. The richness of this history, myth and lore should not be ignored by modern poets, whether they are an enterprising romantic, an observer of events, a political activist or a spiritual/religious wordsmith. Yes, be one a modern animist, a studious Christian, a contemplative Buddhist or of any of the world's faiths – even atheism – the Muse calls to all.

The Basic Styles of Poetry

The basic styles and subjects of poetry and storytelling are widely varied. There are those that follow certain structures and rules, to those that are completely open, with no rules whatsoever. Those styles are sometimes determined by one's country or culture of origin. Others are the invention of classic authors. I will give here a few examples:

Limerick: A five line humorous and/or witty poem that rhymes.

Haiku: An ancient Asian very short style poem that can range from humorous to profound.

Sonnet: A fourteen-line poem that rhymes, as used and further developed by Shakespeare.

Couplet: A double line rhyming poem that can stand alone or be part of a longer poem.

Narrative: A poem that tells a story in short or long form and usually about an event.

Free Verse: Written without any constrictions or rules from mind to pen to paper.

Epic Narrative: A lengthy poem usually in many verses that tells and extols the adventures of a legendary hero or heroes or historical type event.

There are also eulogies and odes to people and events that are most often in poetic form. Also, the poem that becomes lyric is set to music or may be expressed in chanting, which usually is a spoken or semi-spoken form, as in a hymn or a spiritual rite. Hip-Hop, Rant/Slam poetry grew out of New Wave and Modern Rap. Tap birthed Stomp, where again the rhythms that pour from our feet, hands and mouths define generations. In our time, there are so many styles and structures that catch the eye on the written page. Almost endless poetic offerings can be accompanied by photographs, paintings, music, drawings, and even film; the human imagination becomes a reflection of our ever-changing creative universe.

Better Known Cultural Influences on Poetry Throughout Written Time

1.Egypt's New Kingdom (1539-1075 B.C.)

2.The Greek and Roman inspirations, beliefs and thoughts

3. Beliefs of the Norse, Celts, Gauls, Saxons and other Western tribes and cultures. These local cultures included the folkways of those collective families throughout Europe.

4. Many people emigrated to America, bringing their faith and customs with them. Those aspects thereafter mixed with Native American and African lore to create unique spoken poetry and music.

5. The influence of both Eastern and Christian mysticism and its writing.

6. Shakespeare, Arthurian lore and the dawning of the metaphysical poets.

7. The coming of the Theosophists, the Golden Dawn, and the Occult Poets.

8. The Beat, Jazz and Hippie generations.

9. Poets born after World War II became a driving metaphysical force for the 1960's and beyond.

A Brief List of Influential and Famous Poets:

King David	approx. 1100–900 BCE
Homer	1100 BC
King Solomon	970BC – 928 BC
Sappho	630BC – 570 BC
Corinna	500 BC
Ovid	43BCE – 17CE
Aeschylus?	525BC – 431BC
Consort Ban Jieyu	48 BC – 06BC
Ban Gu	32 – 92[1]
Ts'ai Yen	200
Kalidasa	450 – 600
Kakinomoto N hitomaro	662 – 710
Li Bai	701 – 762
Lady Murasaki Shikbiu (??Shikibu??)	973 – 1025
Gormley	1000
Omary Khayyam	1021 – 1122
Duke of Aquintane Guillaume IX	1071 – 1126
Hildegard Von Bingen	1098 – 1179
Mahadeviyakka	1200 –
Rumi	1207 – 1273
Dante degli Aligheiri	1265 – 1321
Lovato Lovati	1241 – 1309
Albertino Mussato	1261 – 1329
Geoffrey Chaucer	1343 – 1400
Torquato Tasso	1544 – 1595
William Shakespeare	1564 – 1616
Mairi Macleod	1569 – 1674
John Milton	1608 – 1674
Sophia Elisaleet Brenner	1659 – 1739
Ono no Komachi	1735 – 1840

---

[1] *Hereafter dates are Anno Domine (AD)*

Cornelia Benavidez

Robert Burns	1759 – 1799
William Blake	1757 – 1827
William Wordsworth	1770 – 1850
Samuel Taylor Coleridge	1772 – 1834
Robert Southey	1774 – 1843
Lord Byron	1788 – 1824
Ralph W. Emerson	1803 – 1882
Alfred Tennyson	1809 – 1892
Emily Dickenson	1830 – 1886
Elizabeth B. Browning	1806 – 1861
Henry Wadsworth Longfellow	1807 – 1882
Edgar Allen Poe	1809 – 1849
Walt Whitman	1819 – 1892
Emily Bronte	1818 – 1847
Charlotte Bronte	1816 – 1855
Aleksey Konstantinovich Tolstoy	1617 – 1875
William Forster	1818 – 1882
Dante Gabriel Rossetti	1828 – 1882
Lewis Carroll	1832 – 1898
Louisa May Alcott	1832 – 1888
Algernon Charles Swinburne	1837 – 1909
Oscar Wilde	1854 – 1908
Emily P. Johnson Tekahionwake	1861 – 1914
Whitcomb Riley	1849 – 1916
Robert Louis Stevenson	1850 – 1894
Khalil Gibran	1883 – 1931
William Butler Yeats	1865 – 1939
Rudyard Kipling	1865 – 1936
Rainer Maria Rilke	1875 – 1926
James Joyce	1882 – 1941
Robert Frost	1874 – 1963
Carl Sandburg	1878 – 1967
John Robinson Jeffers	1887 – 1962
Cesar Vallejo	1892 – 1938
Tekkan Yosana	1883 – 1935
Ezra Pound	1885 – 1972
Edna St. Vincent Millay	1892 – 1950
E. E. Cummings	1894 – 1962
Robert Graves	1895 – 1985
Clark Ashton Smith	1893 – 1961

Elizabeth Bishop	1911 – 1979
Robert Hayden	1913 – 1980
Dylan Thomas	1914 – 1953
Wislawa Szymborska	1923 – 1960
Robert O'Hara	1926 – 1966
Krishna Murthy Sastry	1866 – 1960
Alejandra Pianik	1936 – 1972
Frederick James Wah	1939 –
Homero Aridjis	1940 –
Sharon Olds	1942 –
Cecilia Vicuna	1947 –
W.H. Auden	1907 – 1973
William S. Burroughs II	1914 – 1997
Julia Wright	1915 –
Victor Henry Anderson	1917 – 2001
Noemia da Sousa	1927 –
Natasha Trethewey	1966 –
Alice Oswald	1966 –
Jack Kerouac	1922 – 1969
Doreen Valiente	1922 – 1999
Lisel Mueller	1924 –
Allen Ginsberg	1926 – 1997
Maya Angelou	1928 – 2014
Tsegaye Gabre-Medhin	1936 – 2006
Margaret Atwood	1939 –
Kay Ryan	1945 –
Patricia Monaghan	1946 –
Pam Ayers	1947 –
Pablo Neruda	1904 – 1973
André Breton	1896 – 1966
Jennifer Mary Bornholdt	1960 –
Hai Zi	1964 – 1989
Kevin Young	1970 –
Eduardo Corral	1970 –

Closing Words

As school children, we played word games. In college, there are more adult versions of these games, from the mischievous to the profound. It is usually in the arena of our contemporaneous educational journey that we initially learn to create together. Through the passing years of singing, dancing, and performing during various school readings and plays, we learned the value of words on paper, and how they are, or could be, expressed. It is an educational and heartwarming process to share our human experience within one's community and across cultural lines. It certainly expands consciousness. Exploring and sharing our very personal experiences involves our longing for truths and meaning. Here we bring ourselves to the doorstep of spiritual wisdom in its various guises. This also leads to the agreements of law and faith to become possible and binding.

Poetry speaks to our highest ideals and our deepest hopes for the future, not just for ourselves but for all reality itself. We dare to dream that we may live, work, create and love in peace. Such endeavor is the primary means by which poetry becomes prayer, rite and worship. For some, this marks a return to family tribal roots and for others, a lasting and meaningful connection to the earth itself. We have been, at least since the 1800s, and especially in the West, seeking out the fundamental lore and traditions that guided our ancestors' lives. Now, we use everything from inner meditations, mythic romanticisms, imagination and determined dogmas to reconnect to our historical spirituality. Whether we are of mixed heritage and feel drawn to the ways of one ancestor or another or, after much soul searching, we embrace the philosophy and ways of a tribal outlook, or a more typical modern religious practice, either endeavor can lead to a satisfying kinship. Whether alone, or together with like-minded family or friends, be it in a Monastery, Temple, Church, or Coven, one can pursue a way of devotion and practice that honors ancestors, Gods, Goddesses and/or God the Great Spirit. This imbues us with values that we admire, respect, even love and wish to embrace. It is only natural then for us to elevate and celebrate this sense of wholeness and purpose.

Again, I feel our best clues and guideposts that point the way to healthy well-rounded results are found in sacred stories, lore, and poetry. There we find the tools to help us find ourselves and inspire in us the source of who we really are and where our spirit comes from. Storytelling and Poetry, in the mundane world, is the exploration and celebration of ourselves and a means for examining our moral choices. Its true magic in this life is that it can also be the means to extend an invitation to the forces and beings in the Divine world to reveal themselves and their mysteries to us. Therein and thereby, poetry and storytelling become the gateways and paths to one's human refinement.

Cornelia Benavidez

Appreciations and Thanks

It is with much love I must thank my mother and father, Gisela and Gilberto Benavidez. It is through them, and my grandparents, that I have learned the gifts of words and obtained a deep appreciation of all the arts that have lodged themselves within my soul.

To my beloved family and friends that have passed on: you are always in my heart.

To my sister, Sylvia, thank you. You were my partner in childhood, in storytelling, play and life's lessons. We inspire each other to this day in our written quests.

To my cousin Dietrich Cornelius, thank you. Your love and talent for drumming, inspired me, as you too have explored the rhythms of life.

To my oldest childhood friends Betty, Mary and Janet, thank you, you made and make life so interesting, full and lovely.

To my past loves, you know who you are, thank you for moments of tender beauty and lessons learned.

To Rob Miller, a man who had many skills whether as Soldier, Teacher, Editor or Writer and Father. Your kindness will never be forgotten.

To Timothy, for our past early days of inspirations and the lessons learned.

To William (Bill) for your photo help and support with this project.

To Shirley, my brave friend in all our adventures.

To Caroline, Cathy, Kathy P, Charlotte, Diane, Tara, Linda B. for your kind supportive help and Octavia and Susie for being who you are. Martha, Paula and Judy for including me and giving me courage to keeping to going.

Mike for help with computers, pics and for all odds and ends.

To Ben, Shane, Sara for when you showed up at the right time.

To my husband John Doyle, for your love and early editing help.

To Kaitlin for believing in her Mutti.

Thank you to Mike and Linda for your support and for sharing the beauty of your land and making a space in your family and lives for us.

Thank you to Peter Hollinghurst for a wonderful cover.

Thank you, Storm Constantine, Andrew Collins, Neil Rushton, Louise Coquio all who recognize and celebrate the value of written, spoken and sung words throughout our ages.

"Writers know words are their way towards truth and freedom, and so they use them with care, with thought, with fear, with delight. By using words well, they strengthen their souls. Storytellers and poets spend their lives learning that skill and the art of using words well. And their words make the souls of their readers stronger, brighter, deeper."

- Ursula K. Le Guin

About the Author

Cornelia Benavidez was raised in Albion Michigan by a German mother and a Mexican Indian and Spanish father. She grew up with a rich oral history from both sides of her family. She attended and graduated from Albion College with Major studies in Philosophy, Theater and Psychology. She lived in San Francisco for thirty years studying and working with and for various spiritual organizations. Also, with her husband Atty. John Doyle helped found H.E.A.R Hearing, Education and Awareness for Rockers. Also, managed to sing with various bands in many of San Francisco's best venues.

Recent Titles from Megalithica Books

Zodiac of the Gods by Eden Crane

A new interpretation of the Egyptian Dendera Zodiac, this book explores character analysis for each sign, revealing your relationship with the deity presiding over your month of birth. The book also offers a primer for Egyptian magic, focusing upon the deities of the year. The vivid pathworkings enable you to connect with these ancient gods and goddesses, and work with their energy to influence and improve your life, helping you realise your goals and desires.
ISBN: 978-1-912241-03-3 Price: £11.99, $16.50

SHE: Primal Meetings with the Dark Goddess by Storm Constantine & Andrew Collins

The Dark Goddess is unpredictable, dispassionate, cruel, and often deadly. She reflects our deepest desires, fears, hopes and expectations. In this fully-illustrated book, Storm Constantine and Andrew Collins have selected a fascinating range of 34 goddesses, including some who are not so well-known. The pathworkings to meet them and explore their realms will offer insight into these often-misunderstood deities. (This title is also available as a limited edition, numbered hardback.)
ISBN: 978-1-912241-06-4 Price: £12.99, $18.99

The Elemental Magic Workbook by Soror Velchanes

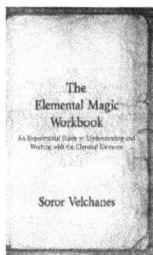

A complete course in elemental magic, providing a solid foundation for future independent work. Explore the nature of each element, how it impacts your life and how you may harness it for personal benefit. Perform elemental rites inspired by various magical tradition, and also develop and perform your own rites. Previous magical experience is helpful but is not required. Everyone is welcome to work with the elements!
ISBN: 978-1-912241-05-7 Price: £11.99, $16.50

www.immanion-press.com

.

www.ingramcontent.com/pod-product-compliance
Lightning Source LLC
Chambersburg PA
CBHW032148080426
42735CB00008B/630

*9 7 8 1 9 1 2 2 4 1 0 8 8 *